THE FAMILY'S SEARCH FOR SURVIVAL

MAN AND CIVILIZATION

THE FAMILY'S SEARCH
FOR SURVIVAL

a symposium edited by

Seymour M. Farber

Piero Mustacchi

Roger H. L. Wilson

University of California
San Francisco Medical Center

McGRAW-HILL *New York   St. Louis   San Francisco*
Toronto   London

MAN AND CIVILIZATION:
THE FAMILY'S SEARCH FOR SURVIVAL

Library of Congress Catalog Card Number 64-23275

*This book is a record of the fourth symposium in the
series "Man and Civilization," held at the University
of California San Francisco Medical Center, January 25
and 26, 1964, and produced in collaboration with
J. Ralph Audy, Louis H. Bell, William J. Brandt,
Barbara Brooks, Gretchen Gause, Sadie S. Kaye, David
G. Mandelbaum, Mary Wakefield, and Jocelyn White,
members of the conference committee. Within the
limits of space, it consists of the actual material as it
was presented. To preserve spontaneity, the panels in
particular have been presented in their original form
with only minor editing. Thus we have as true a
mirror as possible of this unusual symposium.*

CONTRIBUTORS

Nathan W. Ackerman, M.D., Clinical Professor of Psychiatry, Columbia University, New York, New York

J. Ralph Audy, M.B., B.S., Ph.D., Director, Hooper Foundation; Professor of Tropical Medicine and Human Ecology, University of California School of Medicine, San Francisco Medical Center, San Francisco, California

Seymour M. Farber, M.D., Dean of Educational Services and Director of Continuing Education, Health Sciences, University of California San Francisco Medical Center, San Francisco, California

Alvin I. Goldfarb, M.D., Associate Professor of Psychiatry, New York School of Psychiatry, New York, New York

Ping-ti Ho, Ph.D., Professor of Chinese History and Institutions, University of Chicago, Chicago, Illinois

Herma Hill Kay, J.D., Professor of Law, University of California, Berkeley, California

Lester A. Kirkendall, Ph.D., Professor of Family Life, Oregon State University, Corvallis, Oregon

David Krech, Ph.D., Professor of Psychology, University of California, Berkeley, California

Hilda Sidney Krech, Author, Berkeley, California

W. M. Krogman, Ph.D., Professor and Chairman, Department of Physical Anthropology, Graduate School of Medicine, University of Pennsylvania, Philadelphia, Pennsylvania

Judson T. Landis, Ph.D., Professor of Family Sociology, University of California, Berkeley, California

Russel V. Lee, M.D., Executive Consultant, Palo Alto Medical Clinic, Palo Alto, California

Leo Lowenthal, Ph.D., Professor of Sociology, University of California, Berkeley, California

J. Fenton McKenna, J.D., Dean, School of Creative Arts, San Francisco
    State College, San Francisco, California

Donald H. McLaughlin, Ph.D., Regent, University of California

Piero Mustacchi, M.D., Acting Head, Continuing Education in Medicine,
    University of California San Francisco Medical Center, San Francisco,
    California

Talcott Parsons, L.H.D., Dr.Phil., Professor of Sociology, Harvard Uni-
    versity, Cambridge, Massachusetts

James A. Peterson, Ph.D., Professor of Sociology and Chairman, Depart-
    ment of Sociology and Anthropology, University of Southern Cali-
    fornia, Los Angeles, California

Karl H. Pribram, M.D., Professor of Psychiatry and Psychology, Stanford
    University, Stanford, California

C. Easton Rothwell, Ph.D., LL.D., President, Mills College, Oakland,
    California

John B. deC. M. Saunders, M.D., F.R.C.S. (Edin.), Chancellor, Uni-
    versity of California San Francisco Medical Center; Professor of
    Anatomy and Chairman, Department of Medical History and Bibli-
    ography, San Francisco, California

Paul H. Sheats, Ph.D., Dean of University Extension, University of Cali-
    fornia

Neil J. Smelser, Ph.D., Professor of Sociology, University of California,
    Berkeley, California

Roger H. L. Wilson, M.D., Acting Associate Director, Continuing Educa-
    tion, Health Sciences, University of California San Francisco Medical
    Center, San Francisco, California

PREFACE

The present volume offers, in its entirety, the proceedings of a multidisciplinary symposium concerned with the modern family. This is the fourth such symposium, and it is perhaps well to point out again the premise upon which the whole series of symposia, entitled "Man and Civilization," is based: The most imperative necessity laid upon our generation is that we talk together. This book is itself the record of conversations, and it is published in the hope that these conversations can be fruitfully continued.

This is an age of specialization, even in matters of deepest concern to human beings. The study of man is distributed among at least a dozen disciplines, and each discipline has its subdisciplines. There is no need to linger over the manifest advantages of such a distribution of labor; the astonishing accumulation of fact about the human organism in the last thirty or forty years testifies to the value of this approach. But we are inclined to overlook the disadvantages in specialization, which are equally important. The most important disadvantage is that the farther away we move from the whole organism, or even from its major problems, the less able we are to formulate courses of action. We can, for instance, study motivation, social behavior, learning, and so forth, but we can act only in terms of the individual in whom these attributes and capacities inhere, and no one specialist is in a position to act in this fashion. We can confront our human problems constructively only if we learn, somehow, to put our specialized knowledge in the service of general intelligence.

This necessity is particularly apparent, of course, when the subject of the present volume is considered. The uncertain future of the modern family is, of course, generally acknowledged. The family of the nineteenth century derived its strength from the multitude of functions —economic, social, and cultural—that it performed for its individual members. It was the family that provided the only possible financial reserve for its members, even after they had left home; it was the family that determined, for the most part, the social roles available to the individual within it; it was the family, preeminently, that was the entertainment center for its members. This is no longer the case. With regard to social and cultural possibilities, the family is very apt to constitute a limitation upon the potentialities of the individual belonging to it, and its financial support is by no means indispensable. As a consequence, the whole drift of a modern technological society is away from the family as the fundamental social structure.

At the same time, it would seem that no other social structure is able to assume the most important function of the traditional family, the nurture of the young. A child first learns who he is through his relationship to his family, and his mental and moral growth thereafter depends upon the existence of stable and intimate relationships with his elders—relationships which only the family, at the present time, is in a position to provide.

From our present perspective, then, we seem to be witnessing the rapid dissolution of an institution which is yet indispensable. The seriousness of the problem is reflected in the many social sciences centrally concerned with the family and the difficulties that it finds itself in. But, as was pointed out before, the very number of specialists concerned with the problem mitigates against decisive action upon the part of any of them. Furthermore, it is surely obvious that effective decisions upon so momentous a matter must be taken by society itself.

The present symposium was organized in terms of this understanding of the modern family and its problems. It was not designed to be merely a series of reports of new knowledge pertaining to the subject, although much that was new is here made available to the general public for the first time. Rather, it attempts to present, through the most distinguished workers in their several fields, the best knowledge available on the subject in a context which will bring that knowledge to bear upon important choices to be made. The ultimate function of knowledge in human affairs cannot be to relieve human beings of choice; it *can* clarify the choices they must make. This symposium is directed to such clarification.

It is always a pleasure to acknowledge the indispensable contributions by many people which a project of this sort absolutely requires. We are deeply grateful to Chancellor Saunders for his continuous encouragement and advice. The Conference Planning Committee was indefatigable in its efforts to make this a successful and worthwhile event. Our warm thanks must be extended to Dr. Alejandro Zaffaroni, President, and the Syntex Laboratories, Inc., of Palo Alto, for their partial financial support of the program and also of the live telecast. We must also thank television stations KQED, San Francisco, and KVIE, Sacramento, and radio station KXKX, San Francisco, for their excellent production and coverage. Finally, the staff of the Continuing Education Division of the Medical Center was, as usual, quietly magnificent.

Seymour M. Farber
Piero Mustacchi
Roger H. L. Wilson

INTRODUCTION

John B. deC. M. Saunders

Dr. Saunders' early interests in surgery expanded into the fields of anatomy and medical history. His Leonardo da Vinci on the Human Body and works on Vesalius and Egyptian medicine have received great attention. A scholar with wide interests, he has encouraged the increasing breadth of scientific and humanistic endeavor at the San Francisco Medical Center.

Under the general title of "Man and Civilization" there have been held on the San Francisco campus of the University of California a series of symposia. Their purpose has been to explore contemporary problems which relate or misrelate man as a biological and social organism to an environment which, under the pressures of an increasing urbanization, is undergoing swift and dynamic changes.

The further purpose of these symposia is to bring together on a more representative scale members of the scientific and biological disciplines with leaders of religion, philosophy, government, history, literature, and law to examine and discuss problems of the future and suggest appropriate action. It is hoped that such meetings will correct the "overtechnicization" which has characterized the sciences in recent years and assist in strengthening the common bonds of communication between the sciences and the humanities, leading to a unity in cultural aims.

It is most appropriate that discussions between the sciences and the humanities be centered on a campus devoted to the health sciences. First of all, a physician is by tradition and training a man of two worlds whose roots are scientific and whose endeavors humanistic. In ancient tradition, medicine symbolized this dual relationship not in Aesculapius but in Apollo, son of Zeus and Leda, who presided over its broader and public activities as patron of all matters affecting the physical and social, together with the intellectual and moral, affairs of man.

> All harmony of instrument or verse
> All prophecy, all medicine are mine,
> All light of art or nature . . .

says Shelley in his "Hymn of Apollo."

Secondly, the special topic of this symposium, "The Family," is of the greatest importance to the physician in his professional capacity. Although through training and necessity the practicing physician is most concerned with the individual, he is so often made aware of the powerful forces revealed under the stressful conditions of family life that he is constrained to regard the family itself as a veritable organism. "Like father, like son" has more than genetic meaning. Moreover, organism implies order, discipline, and authority so that the part is integrated with the whole, and it is perhaps the meaning of this order and its significance which is the primary subject of discussion in this symposium.

Perhaps in our discussion we shall encounter considerable difficulty in defining what we mean by the generalized term "family," which has many different connotations in the spectrum of human social organization, ranging all the way from concepts of the family as a biological breeding unit to a political or religious institution. Further, since cultural growth implies change, which is enormously accelerated with a rapidly advancing technology, we shall have to look to those measures which indicate the degree of responsiveness and flexibility in our culture if we agree that the preservation, stability, and development of a civilization is dependent upon the harmony between the duration of the individual life cycle and the rate of change.

To discuss these many aspects of the nature of the family and its changing role in the presence of ever-accelerating technological advances, this symposium brings together a group of most distinguished scholars whom we welcome with the words uttered by Tristram Shandy's philosopher father to Uncle Toby in a fraternal squabble over Aunt Dinah's affair with the coachman: "What is the character of a family to an hypothesis?"

CONTENTS

PART ONE

IS THE FAMILY NECESSARY?

Chairman: Paul H. Sheats

A nationally known educator and administrator in California, Dr. Sheats is a former member of the UNESCO National Commission and is now a member of the Board of Directors of the National University Extension Association. He has published numerous articles on adult education.

The symposium opened with its first session devoted to a candid reappraisal not so much of the role of the family but of whether it does in fact have a significant part to play in contemporary civilization. The first paper approached this from a legal and a socio-anthropologic viewpoint, evaluating how the laws of society weaken and strengthen family structure and how the nature of community substitutes for family function. The Chinese family was the next aspect, considered in terms of the extraordinary changes between the overriding family of the past and its contemporary (perhaps transient) disruption in Mainland China. The sociologic approach was considered next, and the relative permanence of a fundamental value of the family as a unit became apparent. The panel which followed expanded on the theme of social structure and persistence of the family as a recognizable phenomenon, despite such apparently destructive approaches as the commune, divorce, and increasing protection of children by the community.

THE OUTSIDE SUBSTITUTE FOR THE FAMILY

Herma Hill Kay

Interested in the application of anthropology to law, Professor Kay is currently at the Center for Advanced Study in the Behavioral Sciences, Stanford, California, where her research is on the relationships of these fields to the family.

For some time social scientists have been calling attention to the changing nature of the American family. Some have discussed the problem in terms of a loss of function within the family. Thus Ogburn [1] listed in 1938 seven functions originally performed by the family (economic, status-giving, educational, religious, recreational, protective, and affectional) and concluded that "at least six of the seven family functions have been reduced as family activities in recent times" [2], while only the seventh, the affectional function, remains vigorous. In 1949 Murdock [3] isolated four functions of the nuclear family—sexual, economic, reproductive, and educational—and found that the family as thus defined is a universal human social grouping, a conclusion that has since been disputed [4]. Even this limited definition of the family's functions has not escaped the challenge of changed conditions. Both the anthropologist Linton [5] and the sociologist Parsons [6] have reduced the functions of the modern nuclear family to two: to socialize children and to provide psychological and emotional security for adults [7]. Neither Linton nor Parsons views this specialization of the family with undue alarm. Indeed, both have separately concluded that the nuclear family is needed to perform these two essential functions for society and that it will survive to fulfill them. The loss of other functions is expressly viewed by Parsons as a transitional stage in family development leading to a basic change in family structure [8].

A social change so basic that it produces a different structure in the American family must also be basic enough to be reflected in the American legal system because the law constantly deals with cases that test the limits of, and set the boundaries for, social institutions. The hypothesis that the customs and values highly prized by a people are reflected sooner or later in its legal system is neither original nor startling. The converse, that values and customs that have lost their cultural significance will be dropped from the legal system either formally, by repeal or reversal, or informally, by nonenforcement, is similarly commonplace. The interesting result of these propositions, however, is to "regard and study the law simply as a great anthropological document," as Oliver Wendell Holmes suggested a good many years ago. Perhaps by turning to American family law, tracing the recent history of changes in that law that have resulted in a reorganization of the legal structure of the family, and then looking for the lines of current development that may lead to still further changes in the future, we may gain some insights that will be useful to behavioral scientists working with the family.

The legal materials [9] indicate that the structure of the family in Anglo-American law has changed since the beginning of the nineteenth century from a patrilineal authority system to a bilateral system based on equality of the spouses. Because the law deals by and large with individuals instead of groups, the legal image of the common-law pre-nineteenth-century family must be pieced together by examining two of the diadic relationships within the nuclear family: first, the relationship between husband and wife and, second, the relationship between parent and child.

The common law defined the husband-wife relationship by suspending the legal personality of the wife. Prior to her marriage, a single woman had the same rights with respect to property, contracts, and capacity to use the courts as did a man. But upon her marriage, as Blackstone puts it, "the husband and wife are one person in law; that is, the very being or legal existence of the woman is suspended during the marriage, or at least is incorporated and consolidated into that of the husband" [10]. This principle is often stated colloquially another way:

At common law, the husband and wife were one, and that one was the husband. The ramifications of this doctrine were many and varied. In the first place, and generally speaking, the wife lost ownership of her personal property and control of her real property. Simply by virtue of the marriage, the husband became the owner of his wife's possessory personal property. He was entitled to its possession during his life and on his death it passed to his estate. The wife was, however, permitted to keep her "paraphernalia," that is, her clothing, jewels, and articles of convenience suitable to her rank after her husband's death, provided his creditors did not require them for the payment of his debts. The husband was also entitled to his wife's "choses in action," including her stocks and bonds, bills of exchange, debts owed to her, and her rights of action at law if he took active steps to reduce them to his possession intending to make them his own. Finally, although the husband did not own the wife's real property, he was entitled to the use of her lands during the marriage. If a child was born to the couple alive and capable of inheriting the wife's land, then the husband was entitled to the use of the land during his life as tenant by the curtesy. The wife, acting alone, had no power to sell or transfer her land.

A second consequence of the wife's loss of legal personality was her inability to make contracts and use the courts. Her contracts were absolutely void, and she was not bound by them unless her husband had been banished from the realm, had left voluntarily, or had been imprisoned for a term of years. Moreover, she could not sue or be sued in a court of law unless her husband was joined with her as a party.

A third consequence of the legal unity of husband and wife was that the husband was liable for his wife's torts (but not her voluntary crimes). Because husband and wife were one legal person, they could not sue each other for damages for wrongful acts committed by one of them against the person of the other.

In addition to positive legal disabilities, the common law emphasized the wife's inferior legal position negatively by denying her the right to recover damages in two situations where that right was granted to the husband. If there was a common accident in which both spouses were injured and rendered incapable of marital intercourse, the husband would have had an action for the loss of consortium but the wife would not. And if the wife was enticed away from the husband by a third party, he would have had an action for the alienation of her affections, but similar relief would not have been available to her under like circumstances.

Finally, the husband had the power to choose the family domicile and its mode of living. He had the duty of supporting his wife, and he could select the means and place at which his duty should be performed. The wife's unreasonable refusal to follow the husband wherever he chose to go constituted desertion.

The husband's paternal authority over his children was another illustration of his legal primacy over his wife. The parent-child relationship at common law was really a father-child relationship. The mother's rights were subordinate to those of her husband, and in many cases her rights arose only if his had been terminated by death. During his life, the father had virtually an absolute right to the custody and control of his minor children, and upon his death he could appoint for the child a guardian whose right to custody was recognized as superior to that of the mother. If he did not appoint a guardian, the mother succeeded to his parental rights.

Other aspects of the father-child relationship at common law illustrated the paternal structure of the family. Thus, the father was entitled to his child's services, and he could demand that the child work for him without pay. If the child worked for an outsider, the father was entitled to his earnings. Partly because of this paternal ownership of the child's services and earnings, the father's rights in his child were stated by the California Supreme Court in 1900 [11] to come within the constitutional provisions for the protection of property. The father's duty to support his children, however, was held in England and some American states to be only a moral obligation not directly enforceable by the child. If the father refused to provide for his child, the poor laws authorized the municipal authorities to do so and then demand reimbursement from the father to the extent of his ability. The father could disinherit the child by will, and the child was unable to obtain a support order against the father's estate. In contrast to the father's absolute right to the child's earnings, however, he had no rights at all to the child's other property.

The immunity from suit for wrongful acts that obtained between husband and wife also extended to parent and child, but the reason was different. There was no theoretical merging of the child's legal personality with that of his parent. Instead, the child's inability to sue the father for torts was based on an unwillingness to permit such a direct challenge to the father's authority in the home. For torts committed against the child by outsiders, however, the father had a right to recover damages just as he could recover for injuries to his horse or cow.

Finally, the parent had the right to punish his child in a reasonable manner—a right that even the common law never gave the husband over his wife's person. This power to correct the child could be delegated to the child's teacher or other persons filling a parental role for the child.

The development of American family law from 1850 to the present is virtually synonymous with the history of the emergence of the married woman as a legal personality. In general, the disabilities of marriage imposed upon her by the common law have been removed by legislation or judicial opinion while her rights as a mother have become equal, if not superior, to those of her husband as a father. The first major reform was legislative: beginning with Mississippi in 1839, every state enacted statutes known as Married Women's Acts to alleviate the harsh property rules of the common law. By and large, the statutes provide that real and personal property owned by a woman at the time of her marriage remains her separate property, and that all property acquired by her after marriage, including her earnings, becomes her separate property. In California and the other six states that follow the civil-law system of marital property, the earnings of both husband and wife are community property [12]. Although it was not until 1951 that a married woman in California was permitted to manage and control her own earnings [13], she has had the right to prevent her husband from giving away the community personal property since 1891 [14] and from conveying the community real property since 1917 [15]. Furthermore, partly as a result of judicial interpretation of the Married Women's Acts, the wife is now permitted to resort to the courts as freely as an unmarried woman, and her husband no longer need be joined with her as a party to the action.

Married women may now contract freely with their husbands as well as with outsiders, but, generally speaking, the husband is not liable for his wife's contract debts unless he has agreed, expressly or impliedly, to meet her obligations. On the other hand, the Married Women's Acts did not terminate the husband's duty to support his wife. Thus, when she contracts for food, clothing, home furnishings, and the like, called "necessaries" by the law, he is liable for the reasonable value of the articles supplied to the family.

Removal of the doctrine of spousal immunity from tort—the rule that since the spouses are one person in law they cannot sue each other for personal wrongs—has largely been a judicial task. Like other judicial reforms, it has proceeded slowly. The 1962 California case, called by a delightful quirk of circumstance *Self v. Self* [16], that abolished the doctrine for this state was able to cite in its support only eighteen other states that had also done away with the prohibition. Indeed, one of those states had seen its judiciary promptly reversed by the legislature, which reenacted the common-law rule.

Many states have abolished the husband's actions for alienation of affections and loss of consortium, thus ending the common-law discrimination against the wife. The recent California case law on loss of consortium illustrates the change in judicial attitude toward the husband's position in the family. In 1958 a wife sued to recover for the loss of consortium arising from an injury to her husband when the taxicab in which he was riding collided with a train. The trial court in effect held that she had no cause of action, and the Supreme Court upheld the judgment, stating that if the common-law rule was to be changed, the legislature should change it [17]. But in 1960, when a husband sued to recover for the loss of his wife's consortium, the Supreme Court reversed a judgment in his favor based on the common-law rule, stating that "drawing a distinction between spouses on the ground that the husband, unlike the wife, had a right of recovery at common law would be extremely inequitable and, further, would ignore the fact that recognition of his right was based upon the wife's subservient position in the marriage relationship whereas, under present-day law, spouses are generally regarded as equals" [18].

The husband still retains his titular position as head of the family and his right to choose a reasonable domicile for the family. But a growing body of cases declaring that it is unreasonable for the husband to expect his wife to share their home with his mother perhaps indicates the law's preference for equality between the spouses in the family group [19].

The recent history of the development of parent-child law again indicates the mother's strengthened legal position in the family. In nearly all states the mother's right to custody of her children has been made equal to that of the father. In some states, as in California, the statutes expressly give the mother preference where the child is very young if the parents are otherwise equally qualified to care for the child [20]. California balances this preference for the mother, however, by preferring the father "if the child is of an age to require education and preparation for labor and business" [21]. The California statute declaring that mother and father are equally entitled to the child's services and earnings [22] is typical of other state laws, as is the provision that neither parent may appoint a guardian for the child without the consent of the other [23].

This enlargement of the mother's rights, however, has so far simply meant that the common-law paternal property right in the child has now become a parental property right. The child himself still occupies nearly the same position he held at common law. The major exceptions to that statement are found in the support laws. The child's legal right to support from both his parents is now recognized, and in some cases he may compel support from his parents' estate. This last right, however, is not well established as yet, and the parental power to disinherit the child is undiminished.

Another exception in California law dealing with the child's earnings illustrates a growing protection of the child against the parent. Hollywood has frequently employed child actors whose salaries at common law would have been the property of their parents. But because minors, like married women, were not bound by their contracts at common law, they could repudiate contracts of employment at will. After several bad experiences, the Hollywood studios secured legislation providing that a minor's contracts for the performance of artistic or creative services could not be repudiated if approved by a court [24]. The statute also provides, however, that the court may withhold approval of the contract until the child's parent or guardian agrees to set aside not more than one-half of the child's earnings for the child's benefit [25]. Thus, the parents of child actors are effectively prevented from exploiting their children for their own profit, even though the California law still states unqualifiedly that the child's earnings are the property of his parents.

This brief survey of the family-law materials indicates a shift from a patriarchal family structure to one in which the spouses are more nearly equal as between themselves but dominant in their legal relations with their children. There are indications, however, that the future path of legal development will be directed toward the emergence of the child as a person in his own right. Thus, in child-custody cases, the prevailing standard for awarding custody is the best interests of the child. If one of the parties seeking custody is a parent, however, and the opposing party is a nonparent, the best interests of the child are presumed to be satisfied by granting custody to the parent unless he is demonstrably unfit to rear the child. Since "unfitness" has come to mean moral unfitness, the presumption in favor of the parent is rarely overcome. Some movement to abolish this so-called "dominant parental right doctrine" in the law of custody can be detected among judges and practicing lawyers [26]. If this were done, facts bearing on the child's needs would be considered first rather than facts establishing the good or bad character of the parent. The child would thus be treated less like the property of his parents and more like an individual.

Although we have been discussing family law, it is interesting to note that the law nowhere defines a family. As we have seen, family problems have been viewed as husband-wife or parent-child problems. The last legal development I wish to discuss today is the growing movement to treat the family as a unit and its problems as group problems. This idea grew out of experience with the juvenile court and its philosophy of protecting and rehabilitating children instead of punishing them. Thus, in California, when a child is referred to the juvenile court for the commission of an act which, had it been committed by an adult, would have been a crime, there is no trial by jury in an adversary setting to determine guilt and assess a penalty, as there would be in an adult criminal case. For example, if a minor is picked up by the police for stealing a car and sent to juvenile hall, the probation officer will secure a social study of the child, his family, and his background. The probation officer then may file a petition on behalf of the minor—not one adverse to him—setting forth the facts that indicate that the minor has stolen the car and thus comes within the juvenile court's jurisdiction. At a hearing before the juvenile court judge where the minor and his parents may be represented by counsel, a determination whether the minor comes within the court's jurisdiction is made. If the determination is in the affirmative, the court considers the social study and decides whether to place the child with a family of good character, in a foster home, a child-care institution, a public agency organized to care for children, or a county juvenile home, ranch, camp, or forestry camp. Throughout the proceedings and the subsequent treatment, the emphasis is on helping the child to become a valuable member of society.

The conclusion drawn from the juvenile court experience by some who have worked with it is that the problems there encountered are family problems. The notion of establishing a family court, with jurisdiction over all affairs of the family, has begun to emerge. Thus, the family court would handle cases involving consent to child marriages, annulment of marriage, divorce and alimony, judicial separation, child support, paternity, child custody, adoption, and juvenile court matters. The court would be assisted by a staff of social workers, psychologists, psychiatrists, and doctors. Information gathered about the court's "clients" would be kept in one place and be made available to the court either in the form of testimony by the social worker or a written report.

It has been suggested that the family court, like the juvenile court, should be freed from the hostility of the adversary process, particularly in divorce and child-custody cases. In counseling sessions with staff specialists an atmosphere of seeking the best interests of the family can be established. But if attempts at reconciliation or settlement fail, the parties are relegated to the more hostile atmosphere of the courtroom. This situation cannot be remedied unless the notion of fault in divorce is eliminated. Briefly, the point is that in legal theory divorces are granted to an innocent spouse as relief from the wrong committed by the guilty spouse. In most states no divorce can be granted unless the fault of the defendant and the innocence of the plaintiff are proved. It goes without saying that divorces are usually the "fault" of both spouses. And it is an open secret that when the parties agree to disagree they can avoid this legal doctrine by the simple expedient of the uncontested divorce. Against this background, a leading California case [27] permitted the granting of divorces to both spouses, thus holding both parties guilty, and pointed out that society would be better served by encouraging both husband and wife to speak freely so that their interests can be evaluated in an atmosphere of truth rather than falsehood.

The law's growing emphasis on the individuality of the persons who make up the nuclear family on the one hand and its tendency to treat their specific problems as group problems on the other seem basically sound. If the family structure is firm, the transfer of family functions to other institutions need not be of undue concern. Indeed, the law itself has reflected to some extent the loss of family functions. Thus, a recent California case held that parents could not remove their children from the public schools for education at home unless the parent acting as teacher held the proper state credentials for instruction in each course the child received at home [28]. Zoning ordinances prohibit the carrying on of certain business activities in residential districts. Although clothing can still be made in the home, it is doubtful whether cotton can be grown in the back yard. The important point to be made, however, is not what the family has lost but rather what the family can become. We have seen that the law is beginning to provide a foundation for the building of a family relationship that considers the needs of each person on a substantially equal basis as well as the interaction of each with the others. I do not know whether the conclusion logically follows from these materials that the family is necessary. I think it does follow, however, that the family is alive and healthy, and given that, and human optimism, I think the family will survive.

References

1. William F. Ogburn, "The Changing Functions of the Family," in Robert F. Winch (ed.), *Selected Studies in Marriage and the Family,* New York, Holt, Rinehart and Winston, Inc., 1953, pp. 74–80.
2. *Ibid.,* p. 75.
3. George P. Murdock, *Social Structure,* New York, The Macmillan Company, 1949, pp. 1–13.
4. Melford E. Spiro, "Is the Family Universal?—The Israeli Case," in Norman W. Bell and Ezra F. Vogel (eds.), *A Modern Introduction to the Family,* New York, The Free Press of Glencoe, 1960, pp. 64–75. E. Kathleen Gough, "Is the Family Universal?—The Nayar Case," in

ibid., pp. 76–92. William N. Stephens, *The Family in Cross-cultural Perspective,* New York, Holt, Rinehart and Winston, Inc., 1963, pp. 12–32.

5. Ralph Linton, "The Natural History of the Family," in Ruth N. Anshen (ed.), *The Family: Its Function and Destiny,* New York, Harper & Row, Publishers, Incorporated, 1959.

6. Talcott Parsons and Robert F. Bales, *Family, Socialization and Inter-action Process,* New York, The Free Press of Glencoe, 1955.

7. Linton speaks of "satisfying the psychological needs of the individuals who enter the marital relationship" (*op. cit.,* p. 49), while Parsons' phrase is "stabilization of the adult personalities of the population of the society" (*op. cit.,* pp. 16–17).

8. Parsons and Bales, *op. cit.,* p. 9.

9. Unless otherwise noted, the legal materials on which this paper is based are summarized in Joseph W. Madden, *Handbook of the Law of Persons and Domestic Relations,* St. Paul, Minn., West Publishing Company, 1931. See also Henry H. Foster, Jr., "Family Law in a Changing Society," in F. James Davis et al. (eds.), *Society and the Law,* New York, The Free Press of Glencoe, 1962, pp. 227–263; and Karl N. Llewellyn, "Behind the Law of Divorce," in *Selected Essays on Family Law,* Association of American Law Schools, Brooklyn, N.Y., The Foundation Press, Inc., 1950, pp. 27–96.

10. 1 Blackstone, *Commentaries on the Law of England,* 442; 2 Id. 433.

11. *In re Campbell,* 130 Cal. 380, 62 Pac. 613 (1900).

12. California Civil Code §§162, 163, 164.

13. California Civil Code §161c.

14. California Civil Code §172.

15. California Civil Code §172a.

16. *Self v. Self,* 58 Cal.2d 683, 376 P.2d 65, 26 Cal. Rptr. 97 (1962). See also the companion case, *Klein v. Klein,* 58 Cal.2d 692, 376 P.2d 70, 26 Cal. Rptr. 102 (1962).

17. *Deshotel v. Atchison, T. & S.F. Ry. Co.,* 50 Cal.2d 664, 328 P.2d 449 (1958).

18. *West v. City of San Diego,* 54 Cal.2d 469, 477, 353 P.2d 929, 6 Cal. Rptr. 289 (1960).

19. See Anno., Acts or omissions of spouse causing other spouse to leave home as desertion by former, 19 A.L.R.2d 1428, 1456–1458 (1951).

20. California Civil Code §138.

21. *Ibid.*

22. California Civil Code §197.

23. California Probate Code §1403.

24. California Civil Code §36.

25. California Civil Code §§36.1, 36.2.

26. See, e.g., Justice Shauer's dissenting opinions, concurred in by Chief Justice Gibson, in *Roche v. Roche,* 25 Cal.2d 141, 152 P.2d 999 (1944) and *Stewart v. Stewart,* 41 Cal.2d 447, 260 P.2d 44 (1953); Henry M. Fain, "Custody of Children," in 1 *The California Family Lawyer,* Berkeley, Calif., Committee on Continuing Education of the Bar, 1961, pp. 587–589.

27. *DeBurgh v. DeBurgh,* 39 Cal.2d 858, 250 P.2d 598 (1952).

28. *In re Shinn,* 195 Cal. App.2d 683, 16 Cal. Rptr. 165 (1961).

AN HISTORIAN'S VIEW OF THE CHINESE
FAMILY SYSTEM

Ping-ti Ho

A renowned expert on early modern and modern Chinese history, Dr. Ho's extensive studies appear in his books, The Ladder of Success in Imperial China: Aspects of Social Mobility, 1368–1911, *and* Studies on the Population of China, 1368–1953. *He is particularly interested in Ming-Ch'ing institutions.*

Ever since the opening of China in the 1840s, Chinese society has been regarded by Western people as a "familistic" society par excellence. Until recently, we could point to no other civilized society in which the family, together with its kinship superstructure, held so strategic a position in the total society. Yet, today, nowhere else do the family's chances for survival appear slimmer than on the Chinese mainland. While in the West many religious and secular organizations can count on society's moral support in their search for means to strengthen the family, which forces of continual industrialism have weakened, in the Chinese mainland today no one dares to defend the family without running the risk of being publicly condemned as a person of reactionary or "feudalistic" views. If the family on the Chinese mainland is to survive, it will have to withstand not only the impact of similar forces of industrialism but also the onslaught of the monolithic, omnipotent, and omnipresent state. It seems appropriate, therefore, that in a symposium on "The Family's Search for Survival" there should be a paper devoted exclusively to China.

But it is not easily conceivable why such a paper should be presented by an historian of early modern China who, as far as the Chinese
family is concerned, is at best an interested layman. Indeed, not until I
had found a justification in the words of a prominent British anthropologist, Dr. Maurice Freedman of the London School of Economics
and Political Science, did I dare to accept the honor to address this
gathering of distinguished scholars and experts on family affairs. After
paying due tribute to those well-known writers on the Chinese family,
Dr. Freedman remarks:

But it is no disrespect to these scholars to assert now that their work is
incomplete. It is in fact incomplete over the whole historical range. . . . In
other words, it is not merely the Chinese family since 1949 that we are
ignorant about. Political and emotional barriers separate us from the Chinese
mainland at the present; . . . there are other barriers between us and the
China of the past [1].

From an historian's point of view, I should like to make the following general observations on existing works on the Chinese family. First,
chronologically, most of them deal with the period after 1920, and even
those few dealing with the traditional family and kinship system do not
go back much further than the late imperial age. The result is that very
little has been said about the historical evolution of this venerable
Chinese institution throughout the past two thousand years. Second,
geographically, those well-known works on the Chinese family revolution in pre-Communist times usually skip over the vast rural hinterland
and deal mainly with changes in family structure in or near urban
centers. Third, the picture of the traditional Chinese family drawn by
modern writers is based largely on legal and ethical principles; seldom
if ever is it based on the voluminous and wide-ranging historical material in which the researcher naturally finds discrepancies between ideals
and realities. Last, since modern writers concern themselves mostly with
the disintegration of the old family and the emergence of the new, they
tend to overemphasize, sometimes frankly out of necessity, "the harsh
and tyrannical features of the traditional family and its internal tensions
and conflicts" [2].

Within the time allowed, I shall confine myself to a brief critical
analysis of the following: (1) the size of the historical and modern

Chinese family; (2) the different types of kinship organization and the net relationship between the modern-type patrilineal clan and the family; (3) the question as to whether the traditional Chinese family was as patriarchal as is usually believed; and (4) forces of change in the twentieth century and the present state of the Chinese mainland family.

The most economical way to summarize the historical evolution of the Chinese family is to study its average sizes during those few periods of history which yield relatively useful statistical data. The common impression that China has been a land of large families is due primarily to the inability of nineteenth-century Western writers on China to differentiate the family from the clan and to distinguish the high-status families from those of lower social orders. In fact, ever since the impending collapse of the feudal system during the fourth century B.C., China has been a land of small families.

One of the main reforms carried out by statesmen of various contending states during the fourth century B.C. was to sweep away remnants of the feudal land system, transforming feudal serfs into independent small holders and encouraging the setting up of small families. The most successful of these statesmen was the Lord of Shang of the northwestern state of Ch'in, which, as a consequence of his reforms, eventually conquered all other states and founded the first unified empire in Chinese history. Shortly after 346 B.C. the Lord of Shang passed a law by which adult brothers, if they lived under the same roof, were liable to double taxation and *corvée* duties [3]. That this law did have its expected long-range effects on the family structure is best testified to by Chia I (200–162 B.C.), a brilliant and unusually observant scholar-official of early Han:

Forsaking propriety, righteousness, benevolence, and grace, the Lord of Shang devoted himself only to making his state powerful. After his law was enforced for two years, social customs of the Ch'in people already began to deteriorate. Consequently, an adult son of a rich household usually moved out of his father's family and set up his own, and an adult son of a poor household often moved into his wife's family and took up her surname. The son would lend a harrow or hoe to his father as if he were conferring a favor. The wife would immediately curse if her mother-in-law occasionally used her basket or broom. . . . Such sons and their wives loved only their own children and knew of only self-interest. How little difference there is between such people and the beasts [4]!

Shorn of its Confucian moral bias, the above passage may well be an apt description of the worst father-son and in-law relationships in the modern industrial society. Chu-fu Yen, who rose from obscurity to high power and died in 127 B.C., recalled his relations with his family during his long struggling years: "My father would not treat me as a son, [and] my brothers refused to have anything to do with me" [5]. We have ample evidence showing the high incidence of infanticide and the reluctance of the nation, including the ruling class, to observe the twenty-seven-month mourning for a deceased parent—the most important symbol of the later Confucian pseudo-religion of filial duty [6]. It does not seem an exaggeration to say that the Chinese family during the early empires was as small, self-centered, and atomistic as that of modern industrial society. In any case, the respectable census of A.D. 2 yields 12,233,062 households and 59,594,978 mouths, giving an average of 4.87 persons per household [7]. It should be noted that by definition and in practice a household was always somewhat larger than a family.

We need to mention only a few more comparatively useful historical figures to show that the average Chinese family has been persistently small in size. The average numbers of persons per household for A.D. 755, 1393, and 1812 are 5.95, 5.68, and 5.33, respectively [8]. Most pre-1949 sample surveys show that the average Chinese family in the twentieth century comprised about five persons. The historical and modern figures all testify, therefore, to the elemental fact that the size of the Chinese peasant family was determined primarily by its basic economic needs and by the fiscal burden it bore.

While from the standpoint of size, the family has undergone comparatively little change during the past two thousand years, there have been significant developments in the family superstructure, which is called *tsu* in Chinese and which literally means "clan." Historically there are three different types of *tsu*, of which modern writers on the Chinese family system know only the third and latest. The *tsu* of the ancient feudal nobility, which was patrilineal and based strictly on primogeniture and which petered out by the third century B.C., should not concern us here. It seems pertinent, however, to review briefly the effect of the second type of *tsu* on the revival of family-orientated values and mores.

As has been pointed out earlier, the Chinese family ties were weak during the Ch'in and former Han period (221 B.C.–A.D. 8). Being apprehensive of the possible correlation between weak family ties and social instability, the rulers of former and later Han repeatedly exhorted the nation to practice the Confucian teaching of filial duty. By later Han times (A.D. 25–220), when the imperial authority progressively declined, powerful officials and landed magnates found in these imperial exhortations a most useful pretext for self-aggrandizement. For as long as a man was able to expand his property and to share it with his forebears, brothers, and close and remote collaterals, he could justify himself by the much-distorted and hypocritized theory of filial duty so typical of later Han times [9]. Consequently, men of political and economic influence established their *tsu,* which usually had a large number of retainers, warriors, tenants, and other kinds of social dependents of various surnames appended to the relatively small core of patrilineal kin. Structurally, therefore, these *tsu* differ from the *tsu* of ancient feudal nobility, based strictly on consanguinity and primogeniture, and from the modern type of kinship so well known to us.

During the subsequent period of barbarian invasions and political division, which lasted roughly from A.D. 300 to 600, the most powerful of these *tsu,* numbering a few dozens, dominated the state and became a self-perpetuating aristocracy. They began to decline from the seventh century onward when China was reunited under the centralized T'ang Empire and when the permanently institutionalized competitive civil service examination system broke up their political monopoly.

Since these *tsu* were by nature aristocratic houses, they had little effect, structurally and functionally, on the modern type of patrilineal clan. But they nevertheless fulfilled an important historical mission by disseminating and perpetuating a central Confucian doctrine which through distortion and hypocritization suited their selfish interests so well. In fact, ever since their rise in later Han times members of these *tsu* led the nation in reviving the twenty-seven-month mourning for deceased parents, in sharing wealth and property with brothers and collaterals, and in transforming the doctrine of filial duty into a pseudo-religion [10]. In due course of time these family-orientated values and mores permeated the lower social strata. This, in the last analysis, is the permanent legacy left by the aristocratic *tsu,* a typical product of the long period of political decentralization. It is worth mentioning in passing that for about thirteen centuries since the founding of the first empire, Chinese commoners in general had no kinship organization.

The third or modern type of *tsu* dates back to the middle of the eleventh century, when the hereditary aristocratic houses had become extinct and the society much more mobile under the combined impact of the examination system and the rise of a variegated economy. Recalling the abject poverty of his orphanhood, the famous early Sung statesman Fan Chung-yen (989–1052) in 1050 donated most of his life savings to setting up a charitable estate for his patrilineal kin in the hope that they and their descendants might not suffer destitution in an increasingly competitive society [11]. Since Fan's charitable estate answered a basic social need, it was immediately hailed as a model, from which patrilineal clans of varying strengths and resources have been evolved. The most successfully and elaborately organized clan usually had a permanent fund and property for the maintenance of the ancestral hall, the relief of poor kin, the operation of the clan school, the periodic compilation of clan genealogy, and even subsidy for kin who sought their higher academic degrees at provincial and national capitals. Besides, such a highly organized clan had its head and elected officers who administered common clan affairs, arbitrated intraclan disputes, and served as a cushion between kinsmen and local authorities. It thus performed many of the functions which in other societies would have been performed by various social and religious organizations.

The structure and functions of the post-Sung patrilineal clan being well known, I shall restrict myself to an assessment of the extent to which it has affected the life of the Chinese. In the first place, the kinship system is likely to have been less extensively distributed geographically than is usually imagined. In general, it has been well developed in lower and central Yangtze provinces and in the two southernmost coastal provinces of Fukien and Kwangtung, but distinctly underdeveloped and thinly spread in the northern half of China. This uneven geographic distribution of patrilineal clans may have been due to the fact that the south, particularly the lower Yangtze, has been economically more advanced and academically more successful. To say that the kinship system is common to all parts of China is therefore incorrect.

In the second place, from its very inception in the middle of the eleventh century the kinship system has always had its organizational weakness because its creation and expansion depend primarily on donations by its most successful members [12]. Few donors were as generous as Fan Chung-yen, who gave most of his life savings to his clan as common property. The economic and social milieu in post-Sung China was such that few families could perpetuate their academic and economic success and retain their wealth for more than a limited number of generations. Unless a clan could renew its socioacademic success from time to time, it was bound to become progressively incapable of performing its original functions. Since at any given time bureaucratically and economically successful men constituted a small fraction of the population, well-endowed clans which could function efficiently as corporate units of social structure must have been statistically rather insignificant [13].

Third, it is important to analyze the relationship between the family and the clan. Even when a clan was well endowed and highly organized, the natural family, which consisted of the husband, wife, immature children, and occasionally one or both of the husband's aging parents, constituted a unit of common consumption. The family rather than the clan has always been basic to economic life. There were, of course, clans in which several generations shared property and lived together, but such clans must have been rather rare at any given time, hence invariably extolled by rulers and members of the elite as models. From genealogies, biographies, local histories, and individual literary works it is quite clear that the property owned by the clan, if any, was usually rather small in proportion to the total amount of property separately owned by its various component branches and families: and this despite the fact that the clan property was in principle inalienable because of the necessity to perform certain common clan functions, while the family properties were periodically divided by male heirs who set up their own families. In terms of the most important economic function, therefore, the clan was at best marginal to the average Chinese, whose life was lived within his own small family.

All this does not, however, mean that the patrilineal clan has played no significant role in the life of the Chinese. Politically, a well-organized clan served as a useful intermediary between its members and local authorities. By maintaining the ancestral hall, observing ancestral worship, compiling genealogy, and disseminating Neo-Confucian ethical ideals, the clan certainly helped, at least sentimentally, to strengthen the family and kinship ties. I suspect that it is chiefly by studying these noneconomic and peripheral functions rather than the bookkeeping of highly organized clans, which are statistically insignificant, that modern students have acquired the impression that the Chinese society is familistic and clannish.

To conclude our discussion on the kinship system, I should like to point out its one legacy that has not been noticed. As has been mentioned, the clan was an important instrument for the dissemination of the Neo-Confucian teaching of sharing one's wealth with one's kin. The permeation of this teaching, together with the general insecurity of property and the constant working of social and economic leveling forces, has diluted the concept of property and accounted for the typically Chinese fatalist view that property is inconstant. In this connection, it seems a historical irony that the kinship system, which has been condemned for so long by modern Chinese radicals as "feudalistic," has in fact facilitated the revolution in property ownership in the present Chinese mainland.

The problem as to whether the Chinese family was truly patriarchal may conveniently be examined from two angles: the authority of the family head, who is normally the father, and the status of women.

The authority of the father reflected in traditional Chinese law and ethical precepts is well summarized by a modern writer:

The Chinese family was patriarchal. The grandfather or father was the ruling head and had authority over all the members of the family, including his wife and concubines, his sons and grandsons, their wives and children, his unmarried daughters, his collateral relatives who were junior to him and who shared his domicile, his slaves and servants. His control of the family economy and his power to make financial decisions strengthened his authority. In addition, since the concept of ancestor worship was central to the perpetuation and solidarity of the family, the authority of the family head, who was also the family priest, was further enhanced. Finally, his authority was recognized and supported by the law [14].

If we scratch the dynastic codes deeper, we find in those clauses defining the so-called father's authority that the father is invariably mentioned together with the mother. The authority was therefore not the father's alone but that jointly held by the parents, which by definition included more senior direct patrilineal ascendants. For the basic legal and ethical principle regulating the traditional Chinese family was based not so much on sexes as on senior-junior relationships. This being the case, juniors owed their filial duty to seniors of both sexes. "This elementary consideration alone," writes a British expert on Chinese law, "marks off a clear distinction from the unitary *patria potestas* of the Romans" [15]. This is why throughout Chinese history there have been a number of female rulers, and even down to the early years of the Republic there were still many matriarchs in high-status families [16].

Moreover, although it is a common belief that the Chinese family head had an unrestricted authority to control and dispose of family property, various types of Chinese historical literature and modern Japanese surveys of Chinese customary law reveal a far different picture. Numerous cases can be culled from genealogies and biographies to show that although legally an adult son succeeded his father as the family head, he could not dispose of the family property without the authorization of his widowed mother, who, according to Neo-Confucian precepts, should obey her son. Japanese field surveys of customary law carried out in North China during the last war further reveal that "in many places people would at any rate not buy land from a father unless his sons joined in the conveyance" [17]. Historical literature also shows that in many cases the family property, which was legally in the possession of the family head, was virtually held under a sort of father-son co-ownership or family joint ownership.

Concerning the status of Chinese women, the late Dr. Hu Shih (1891–1962), the greatest scholar of twentieth-century China, had the following to say:

At the outset, it is necessary to point out that the position of women in the old family was never so low as many superficial observers have led us to believe. On the contrary, woman has always been the despot of the family. The authority of the mother and the mother-in-law is very well known. Even the wife is always the terror of the husband; no other country in the world can compete with China for the distinction of being the nation of hen-pecked husbands. Certainly, no other country has produced so many stories of hen-pecked husbands. The wife built up her strong position sometimes upon love, sometimes upon beauty or personality, but in most cases upon the fact that she could not be dislodged from her position: she could not be divorced! It is true that there was no law forbidding divorce; and that the Classics laid down seven conditions for divorcing a wife. Jealousy, or failure to bear sons, or even talking too much, would be sufficient to divorce her. But the same Classics also gave three conditions under which she could not be sent away: (1) if she has shared with the husband a three-year mourning for one of his parents; (2) if the husband has become rich or attained high official positions since marriage; or (3) if she has no home to go back to. These conditions were very common and almost made divorce absolutely impossible [18].

In spite of the very considerable truth in Dr. Hu Shih's observation, it is likely somewhat one-sided; nonetheless, it is invaluable as a corrective to an equally one-sided view that Chinese women have always been cruelly subjected to men.

To get a more balanced view, we have to differentiate the families of higher and lower social orders. Only a high-status family could afford to be large, and hence it would be more prone to have intergenerational and in-law tensions and conflicts, which, shown in legal and ethical precepts on which much of modern scholarship is based, are necessarily exaggerated. In fact, much of the harsh authoritarian character of the Chinese family reflected in law was often mellowed by social customs, human nature, and traditional teachings to curb one's own desires and to consider others' interests. When high-status families are not treated as an abstract theoretical model but as concrete historical examples, cases of tyrannical "patriarchs" must have been rather rare in any period of Chinese history. The low-status family usually was structurally simple and numerically small. Life at this social level depended primarily on the husband's labor, which not even his father could exploit. He thus usually set up his own small family, apart from his brothers and parents. Since he had to toil together with his wife to make ends meet, he did not have even the faintest resemblance to the august head of a high-status family. His wife, if she did not have the material comfort and security of the wife of a high-status family, had more strength as an individual and was much less likely to have an in-law problem.

In fact, even the mores and norms of low-status families differed from those of high-status families. To give only one example, the Neo-Confucian taboo on widow's remarriage has seldom if ever applied to women of lower social orders.

Now we shall assess the changes in the family and kinship system in modern times. Prior to the founding of the People's Republic of China in October, 1949, the family and kinship system had already been weakened by forces and factors such as, for example, the beginnings of industrialization along the eastern seaboard and inland river ports, the improved means of transportation and the more diversified professional opportunities which brought many peasants and intellectuals from their ancestral homes to large urban centers, the new schools and universities which exposed the young to Western ideas and culture, and the so-called renaissance movement from the late 1910s onward which engendered among the intelligentsia a revolt against traditional institutions and family-orientated values.

In the last analysis, it was members of the intelligentsia who were the standard-bearers of the so-called family revolution, which demanded, among other things, the adoption of a single sex standard, the emancipation of women, free choice of mate, and greater freedom for the young. Some of them went so far as to attack even filial duty, which had accounted so much for the family-mindedness of the Chinese. Since the intellectuals came usually from families of higher social orders, in the cities as well as in the country, the movement gradually brought about a liberalization of high-status families throughout the country. But the vast majority of families of the rural hinterland remained little changed. What was most adversely affected by these new forces and ideas was the clan, which was always marginal to economic life and which always depended on the support of its successful members. Since successful men were now mostly urban dwellers susceptible to new ideas, clans in general suffered. In retrospect, perhaps the most striking change in social institutions in pre-1949 China was not the so-called family revolution, because most families were able to hold on, but the fairly rapid decline and disintegration of the kinship system.

One interesting product of this period of change was the Civil Code of 1931, which was partly a crystallization of the ideas of Western-trained intellectuals, partly a compromise with tradition, and partly for foreign consumption because ever since the Washington Conference of 1921–1922 the successive Chinese governments had been working on modern codes in the hope the extraterritoriality might soon be abolished. Such a curious mixture defies precise analysis, but it is a landmark in the history of Chinese law for having established the principle of monogamy, though not without exceptions, and of women's improved status in terms of marriage, divorce, and property. There is no evidence, however, that this code was ever seriously enforced by the Nationalist government.

But there can be no doubt that from its promulgation in May, 1950, to about the end of 1953 the Marriage Law of the People's Republic of China was energetically enforced. Despite its narrow title, it actually amounts to an abbreviated code regulating a wide range of family affairs. It reaffirms or establishes the principle of monogamy; of free choice of partner; of completely equal rights for both sexes as to the management and inheritance of property, choice of occupation, and rearing and educating of children; of divorce upon mutual consent or upon insistence of one party; and of protection of children's interests. So perfect is the symmetry of rights for both sexes that it is high fashion for a married woman to retain her own family name. The law makes a significant concession to tradition by providing that parents and children have the duty to assist each other and to inherit each other's property. Thus the family may, in addition to husband, wife, and immature children, consist of one or both aging parents. In terms of membership, therefore, the law is by no means revolutionary since the majority of families have always been small and only occasionally three-generational.

But functionally the present family is truly revolutionary. As Dr. Freedman ably puts it:

The whole range of activities once covered by the family is now reduced to a narrow field in which husband, wife and children associate together in the interstices, so to speak, of large institutions—the work group, the dining hall, the nursery—which have taken over the functions of economic coordination, housekeeping, and the rearing and educating of children. The family has become an institution for producing babies and enjoying the leisure time left over from the major pursuits of everyday life [19].

What is left to the Chinese family is precious little. We want to ask: can that precious little survive?

Much of the reporting in our press on Chinese family life in the communes is secondhand and too biased to be worth mentioning. Fortunately, there is a firsthand report by a highly trained Canadian child psychiatrist, entitled "The Cheerful Children of Red China's Communes," which says:

I was particularly interested in observing the effects of communal living, a way of life that now involves some eighty percent of all Chinese families. The mother . . . delivers her child to a crèche or nursery in the morning and picks him up at night. In larger towns, members of the family eat all meals in communal dining rooms; sewing, washing, ironing and other household chores are performed by communal service stores. Most Western writers have concluded that this shift in responsibility has disrupted family life to an alarming degree. From my own observations, I don't share this alarm. The old-style patriarchal home is certainly being replaced, especially in the cities, but I don't think the new kind of Chinese home has appreciably weakened family ties. . . . I was impressed by the relaxed, happy relationship of parents and children in the evenings. In the country, the children played or rested nearby as the parents gossiped with relatives and neighbors. In the city, they went together to beautiful public parks that provide outdoor plays, movies, operas, concerts, acrobatics, puppet shows and art exhibits. It seemed to me that these relaxing hours made up, to a large extent, for the lack of contact with the mother during the day. . . . I couldn't help thinking that the day-to-day routine of the Chinese family has much to commend it, compared to that of the family of a Canadian working mother. . . . In some respects, there is greater warmth in Chinese child-parent relationship than there is in Canada [20].

I would not have believed the above report had I not had opportunities to hear similar observations from the ex-cultural attachés of the British and Swedish embassies in Peking, from a French sinologist and his Chinese wife, and from my own relatives.

In my final conclusion, I should like to point out that one of the geniuses of the Chinese people has been their ability to reduce complex things to bare essentials. Well over a thousand years ago they had reduced the thirty or so heavens and the eighteen or so hells of Indian Buddhism into little more than a system of metaphysics and mental hygiene. Today, after more than two thousand years, they have stripped the family of all its functions except one, namely, to procreate, nurture, and educate children with understanding and love, a function which no other human agency can perform. If they have so far succeeded in making this one function work under circumstances many times more difficult than those which confront the Western family, we may perhaps end on a note of guarded optimism: the family will survive.

References

1. Maurice Freedman, "The Family in China, Past and Present," *Pacific Affairs,* 31(4):334, Winter, 1961–1962. This article is, in my opinion, the best analysis of the Chinese family in any language. I am deeply indebted to it for having helped me to better focus my accumulated historical data, which lead to conclusions similar to Dr. Freedman's. The other well-known works on the subject are: Marion J. Levy, Jr., *The Family Revolution in Modern China,* Cambridge, Mass., Harvard University Press, 1949; C. K. Yang, *The Chinese Family in the Communist Revolution,* Cambridge, Mass., The Technology Press of the Massachusetts Institute of Technology, 1959; Francis L. K. Hsu, *Under the Ancestor's Shadow: Chinese Culture and Personality,* New York, Columbia University Press, 1948; Morton H. Fried, *Fabric of Chinese Society: A Study of the Social Life of a County Seat,* New York, Frederick A. Praeger, Inc., 1953; and Olga Lang, *Chinese Family and Society,* New Haven, Conn., Yale University Press, 1946. The two useful works on the Chinese kinship system are: Hsien-chin Hu, *The Common Descent Group in China and Its Functions,* New York, Viking Fund, 1948; and Hui-chen Wang Liu, *The Traditional Chinese Clan Rules,* New York, Association for Asian Studies, 1959.

2. C. K. Yang, *op. cit.,* pp. 20–21.

3. Ssu-ma Ch'ien, *Shih-chi,* Palace ed., Chap. 68.

4. Pan Ku, *Han-shu,* with additional commentaries by Wang Hsien-ch'ien, 1902 ed., Chap. 48, pp. 18b–19a.

5. Ssu-ma Ch'ien, *Shih-chi,* translated by Burton Watson under the title *Records of the Grand Historian of China,* New York, Columbia University Press, 1961, Vol. II, p. 236.

6. Lei Hai-tsung, "Chung-kuo ti chia-tsu chih-tu" (The Family System in Chinese History), *She-hui k'e hsueh* (The Social Sciences, Tsing-hua University), 2:4, July, 1937.

7. Pan Ku, *op. cit.,* Chap. 28, Parts 1–5, *passim.*

8. The figures for A.D. 755 are from Tu Yu, *Tung-tien,* Commercial Press reprint, Chap. 7, p. 41. Figures for 1393 and 1812 are from Ping-ti Ho, *Studies on the Population of China, 1368–1953,* Cam-

bridge, Mass., Harvard University Press, 1959, pp. 55–57. It should be noted that the figure for 1812 covered only fourteen provinces.

9. Since filial duty had by later Han times been generally accepted as the most important yardstick with which to assess one's moral character, many people purposely extended the twenty-seven-month mourning to fantastic lengths—six or more years. Some even observed similar mourning for former official superiors or teachers. The hypocritization of filial duty may best be illustrated by the commoner Chao Hsuan of Ch'ing-chou in central Shantung, who observed mourning for his parents for over twenty years and consequently was hailed by people of his locality as a man of great virtue. However, Ch'en Fan, one of the officials of real integrity, sentenced Chao to prison on the ground that the latter, instead of practicing continence as a genuine practitioner of filial duty, had, during the period of mourning, sired five children. Shortly before the fall of later Han in A.D. 220, K'ung Jung, a descendant of Confucius serving as governor of Tung-hai in modern Hopei, so revolted against the social hypocrisy of his time that he executed a social aspirant because the latter, while wailing full-lunged at his father's burial, showed no real grief. Some members of the ruling class and many more social climbers would relinquish their own shares of family property for their brothers and near kin in order to win social recognition as men of fraternal love. For examples of genuine and false practices during this period of revival of filial duty and family ties, see Chao I, *Nien-erh-shih tsa chi* (Notes on Twenty-two Dynastic Histories), Shih-chieh shu-chu ed., pp. 61–62; and Ch'ien Mu, *Kuo-shih ta-kang* (An Outline of Chinese History), Ch'ang-sha, 1940, Vol. I, pp. 132–36.

10. Lei Hai-tsung, *op. cit.*, and Yang Lien-sheng, "Tung-Han ti hao-tsu" (The Powerful Houses of Later Han), *Ch'ing-hua hsueh-pao* (Tsinghua Journal), 9:4, October, 1936.

11. For the life and career of Fan Chung-yen, see James T. C. Liu, "An Early Sung Reformer: Fan Chung-yen," in J. K. Fairbank (ed.), *Chinese Thought and Institutions*, Chicago, The University of Chicago Press, 1957. For Fan's pioneering clan organization and its historical evolution, see Denis C. Twichett, "The Fan Clan's Charitable Estate, 1050–1760," in David S. Nivison and Arthur F. Wright (eds.), *Confucianism in Action*, Stanford, Calif., Stanford University Press, 1959.

12. In fact, Fan's later contemporaries, especially the famous Neo-Confucian philosophers Ch'eng Hao and Ch'eng I, understood the

basic weakness of the patrilineal kin better than most modern writers. In order to prevent patrilineal kin from suffering an almost inevitable long-range social and economic leveling, they advocated the revival of the ancient feudal type of clan based strictly on primogeniture. Only by so doing, they argued, could the clan property remain locked in the hand of the *tsung-tzu,* i.e., the eldest heir of the eldest legitimate line. But social customs and economic conditions from Sung times onward made the adoption of this proposal impractical.

13. From my own sampling of scores of clan genealogies I have the impression that really well-endowed clans which could perform efficiently their multiple functions were rather few. Genealogies usually list more functions than the mere maintenance of the ancestral hall, but it may be conjectured that only clans of above-average economic means could periodically print their genealogies. The majority of clans do not seem to have been able to manage much more than maintenance of the ancestral hall and observance of ancestor worship. It is interesting to note that in North China few clans had even an ancestral hall or any property. Sidney D. Gamble, in *North China Villages: Social, Political, and Economic Activities before 1933,* Berkeley, Calif., University of California Press, 1963, p. 15, states: "In most villages even the largest family groups were hardly large enough or wealthy enough to have clan halls or clan land. So far as we could observe, such properties were not part of the general pattern in North China."

14. T'ung-tsu Ch'u, *Law and Society in Traditional China,* Paris, 1961, p. 20.

15. H. McAleavy, "Certain Aspects of Chinese Customary Law in the Light of Japanese Scholarship," *Bulletin of the School of Oriental and African Studies, University of London,* 17(3):544, 1955.

16. Lien-sheng Yang, "Female Rulers in Imperial China," *Harvard Journal of Asiatic Studies,* 23:61(esp.), 1960–1961.

17. McAleavy, *op. cit.,* p. 544.

18. Hu Shih, *The Chinese Renaissance,* Chicago, The University of Chicago Press, 1934, pp. 104–105. Copyright (1934) by The University of Chicago Press.

19. Freedman, *op. cit.,* pp. 332–333.

20. Denis Lazure, "The Cheerful Children of Red China's Communes," *MacLean's Magazine,* Mar. 11, 1961.

THE NORMAL AMERICAN FAMILY

Talcott Parsons

One of America's outstanding sociologists, Dr. Parsons is the author of many works on the basic social structure of family and society. Formerly Chairman of the Department of Sociology and Social Relations at Harvard, he is a Fellow of the American Association for the Advancement of Science and a past president of the American Sociological Association.

Of course in the nature of their job social workers encounter a disproportionate sample of the failures and casualties of American family life. There are indeed many such at all levels of the socioeconomic scale, but they are rather heavily concentrated in the lower-income groups, and complicated there by racial and ethnic problems. It is, however, important to see these phenomena, and of course also the problem cases in the upper groups, in the perspective of the total society and its trends of change.

The most important processes of development in American society during the present century, as before, have been continuing differentiation in its structure, a general process of upgrading of expectations and responsibilities, and the related development of new modes of integration of persons and substructures in the increasingly complex society. As a process of very rapid social change, complicated by such external disturbances as hot and cold wars, it is a process marked by much internal disturbance, anxiety, and conflict on many different levels.

The family and its more immediate environment have been centrally involved in the general process, and the end certainly is still far away. Perhaps the best single reference point is to the structural differentiation of the nuclear family, both from other components of the kinship system and from nonkin elements. The most striking case is the performance of occupational roles outside the family in many types of employing organizations. The most massive index of this is the decline of the proportion of the labor force engaged in agriculture, but many other family-operated productive units, like small retail shops and handicraft enterprises, have also been declining in number. With this, of course, has gone dependence of the family household, as consuming unit, on money income, and drastic reduction in its relative self-sufficiency.

The composition of the household has also tended increasingly to be confined to nuclear family members. Thus households with complete nuclear families, i.e., husband, wife, and their own children, increased in proportion of total persons from 80 to 82.7 per cent between 1940 and 1960. During the same period, the proportion of household members who were relatives of the head other than spouse or own children, decreased from 7.7 to 5.5 per cent. The categories of nonfamily members, lodgers, and living-in domestic servants decreased from 4.2 to 1.5 per cent; the domestic-service figure, though small, is particularly striking in decreasing from 0.8 to 0.2 per cent, i.e., being cut to one-fourth in only twenty years. Of course the other side of the picture has been a sharp increase in nonfamilial households, i.e., those composed of single persons or those unrelated, such as two women. The increase in proportions of husbands and wives living together, from 40.5 per cent of total household members to 44.1 per cent, an increase of nearly 10 per cent in twenty years, is particularly striking in the light of the high divorce rate, which remains high though it has tended to decline slowly since the postwar peak. I think the proposition is correct that we now have the largest proportion, in the history of the United States Census, of persons of marriageable age and not widowed living with their spouses and, if the children are not yet too old, with their own children. The broad picture is that of an increasingly specialized but structurally intact family.

This impression of the importance of the family is strengthened by two further facts, namely, the decreasing average age of marriage to a point of near twenty-two for males and twenty for females, and the well-known increased birth rate, which has now been sustained since about 1940—the net reproduction rate for 1959 being a little over 1.7. There have, however, been other crucial changes. One of the most important is the extension of the span of life. Though there has been relatively little change in the last decade or so, since early in the century it has been dramatic. The *average* expectance of life at birth has reached seventy years, though as of 1959 there was a differential of 6.5 years in favor of women over men. A further particularly interesting change is the compression of the childbearing period. Combined with the trend to early marriage, this meant that by 1957 (Glick) the average American mother had her *last* child when she was twenty-six years old, in spite of the higher birth rates. This, of course, means that most married couples face a much longer period of the "empty nest," when their children are independent and neither is widowed, than has previously been the case. The combination of early marriage for girls and the greater longevity of women also means that there is a considerable excess of widows over widowers.

Another important phenomenon of differentiation in the life cycle has been the enormous growth of formal education. There is, first, the extension of full secondary education to all but a decreasing minority, though the dropouts from high school constitute the core of the juvenile-delinquency problem. Second, there is the rapid increase in the college population, running to about 40 per cent beginning some kind of college, and close to 25 per cent completing a four-year college course. Finally, postgraduate professional education, though still small in percentage, is by far the most rapidly growing sector of the educational system. This has occasioned important family problems in that a rapidly increasing proportion marry before completing their formal training.

A final notable set of demographic facts in this area concerns the gainful employment of married women. Between 1950 and 1960 the proportion of single women in the labor force actually declined, presumably because more of them were in school or college. The most striking figure, however, is the increase from 24.8 to 30 per cent between 1950 and 1960 among those living with their spouse, an increase of more than 25 per cent in a decade. The employment of women who were widowed or divorced has, on the other hand, increased much more slowly. Clearly the former increase is associated with the compression of the period of responsibility for the care of small children. It is quite clear, however, that the American woman is more frequently a married woman and probably for a larger fraction of her life than ever before. She is, at the same time, becoming increasingly highly educated and, in spite of the scarcity and expense of domestic service, she is less often "only" a housewife and a volunteer church and community worker than her predecessors. Particularly over the life cycle, her roles have become much more differentiated.

It is of course a commonplace that the American family is predominantly and, in a sense, increasingly an urban middle-class family. There has indeed been, if not a very great equalization of income (though there has been some in the present century), a very substantial homogenization of patterns of life in the population with reference to a number of things. Basic to this are the employment of one or more family members outside the home; the nuclear family household without domestic service except for cleaning and baby-sitting; and the basic constituents of the standard of living, including in particular the familiar catalogue of consumer durable goods, which constitute the basic capital equipment of the household [1].

It can then be said that, in a sense that has probably never existed before, in a society that in most respects has undergone a process of very extensive structural differentiation, there has emerged a remarkably uniform, basic type of family. It is uniform in its kinship and household composition in the sense of confinement of its composition to members of the nuclear family, which is effective at any given stage of the family cycle, and in the outside activities of its members, e.g., jobs for adult men, some participation in the labor force for women, school for children, and various other types of community participation. Indeed it is also highly uniform in the basic components of the standard of living, e.g., the private dwelling, the mechanical aids, the impingement of communications from the outside through the mass media, etc. There is one increasingly conspicuous and distressing exception to the general pattern, namely, the situation of the lowest groups by most of the socio-economic indices, such as income, education, occupational level, etc. This problem will have to be taken up again later.

The author has, perhaps more than anyone else, been responsible for diffusing the phrase "isolated nuclear family" to describe one aspect of this unit. This concept has recently been challenged notably by two groups of sociologists, Eugene Litwack and Melvin Seeman and their associates, in the name of the importance of the network of extended kinship relations beyond the nuclear family. To my mind the two views are not contradictory but complementary. The concept of isolation applies in the first instance to kinship structure as seen in the perspective of anthropological studies in that field. In this context our system represents an extreme type, which is well described by that term. It does not, however, follow that all relations to kin outside the nuclear family are broken. Indeed the very psychological importance for the individual of the nuclear family in which he was born and brought up would make any such conception impossible.

By and large, however, as our population elements are further removed from peasant or other similar backgrounds, these extended kinship elements do not form firmly structured units of the social system. They are not residential or economic units—in the consuming, to say nothing of the producing, sense—nor are they "corporate groups" in the sense that clans and lineages in so many societies have been. There are above all two significant features of their relations to the nuclear family. First, in the maintenance of going relations, though there seems to be clear precedence of members of the families of orientation of both spouses—parents so long as they live, and siblings, even among siblings as between the two families, and much more so beyond that—there is a marked optional quality of the expectation system. There certainly are some structured preferences on kinship bases, and others on those of geographical propinquity, but still there is a strong tendency for kinship to shade into friendship in the sense of absence from the latter of ascriptive components of membership. Hence, the amount of visiting, of common activity, of telephone and written communication, etc., is highly variable within formal categories of relationship. This suggests that extended kin constitute a resource which may be selectively taken advantage of within considerable limits.

This supposition is greatly strengthened by the second consideration. This is the extent to which extended kin, especially members of the family of orientation but not only they, serve as a "reserve" of expectations of solidarity and willingness to implement them which can be mobilized in case of need. To take one primary context, there is a clear expectation that adult siblings, children, and, increasingly, parents of adults will be economically independent and should not need to be the recipients of direct financial aid from relatives. The extended family is, in this sense, normally not a solitary-operating economic unit. In case of special need, however, the first obligation to help, if there is no organized community provision and sometimes when there is, falls on close relatives who are financially able to bear the burden. Such obligations are not likely to be unlimited, but they are none the less real—in cases of sickness, of the dependency of old age, and similar cases.

An interesting case is the one mentioned above. The tendency is for earlier marriage, which, in the most highly educated groups, very frequently occurs before completion of higher education. Not only does this situation give rise to an important part of the employment of younger married women—who thereby earn the fictional degree of P.H.T. ("put hubby through"). There is also a substantial amount of aid from parents and some from older siblings which helps fill the gap. Often this is partially concealed in the form of "gifts," e.g., of a car or a vacation trip, testifying to the importance of the need for "independence." Ritual solidarity on the occasion of weddings, but even more especially funerals, fits in with this pattern.

On this background I may now turn to a few functional and analytical considerations. More than any other influence, psychoanalytic psychology has, during the last generation, made us aware of two crucial things. The first is the fundamental importance for the individual personality of the process of growing up in the intimacies of the family. Not only is mental illness to a large, though by no means exclusive, extent generated in the relations of a child to members of his family [2], but normal personality development is highly contingent on the proper combination of influences operating in the family situation. Of course the family stands by no means alone, and as the child grows older, influences from the neighborhood, then the school and beyond become increasingly important. The family, however, lays the essential foundations and continues always to be important.

There has been a good deal of discussion of the importance of psychological "security" in this whole context. An individual's sense of security naturally depends on his experience in his family of orientation. It remains, however, an essential problem throughout life [3]. We have become increasingly aware that for the adult, in psychologically very complex ways, his family of procreation is dynamically most intimately linked with his family of orientation. The experience of parenthood is of course a recapitulation in reverse of that of the child in relation to his parents, and in important ways reactivates the psychological structures belonging to that period. Just as much, marriage is a complex organization of components in the personality which are derived from childhood experience—the common involvement of eroticism in both is the surest clue to the relationship.

For the normal adult, then, his marriage and his role as parent constitute the primary going reinforcement of his psychological security. The family can thus be seen to have two primary functions, not one. On the one hand it is the primary agent of socialization of the child, while on the other it is the primary basis of security for the normal adult. Moreover, the linkage of these two functions is very close. The point may be put by saying that their common responsibility as parents is the most important focus of the solidarity of marriage partners, and that the desire for children is the natural outcome of a solid "romantic" attraction between two persons of opposite sex. The primary link between these two functions in terms of agency is clearly the feminine role in its dual capacity as mother and as wife.

I think it reasonable to suggest that the broad pattern of the contemporary American family, sketched above in statistical terms, fits this functional analysis. It seems to be a case of a process of differentiation through which the central functions of early socialization and giving individuals a psychological security base have become separated out from others to which they have been ascribed in less differentiated societies. The sharing of the common household as the place to "live" with all its implications is the fundamental phenomenon—it is this sharing which makes the normal nuclear family a distinctive unit which cannot be confused with *any* others, based either on kinship or on other criteria. The home, its furnishings, equipment, and the rest constitute the "logistic" base for the performance of this dual set of primary functions.

The family, however, is not only a setting into which individuals escape from the pressures of the outside society; it also has profoundly important functions in that society. The keynotes to what I have in mind may be stated with reference to two concepts mentioned above, namely that of "reserves" of solidarity and that of basic trust as discussed by Erickson. Following Durkheim, I should say that one of, to me the four, essential conditions of the adequate functioning of a social system is the solidarity among its members. This may be conceived as their motivational readiness to accept their common belongingness as members of a collective system and to *trust* each other to fulfill mutual expectations attached to membership in their respective roles.

The more differentiated and the larger the scale of the social system which depends on solidarity, however, the less can solidarity be dependent on common membership in groups where norms are highly particularistic and the relations rigidly ascribed, and where loyalties are highly diffuse and grounded in immediate affective motivational interests. Thus national community and a highly generalized system of legal norms are foci of organization highly dependent on solidarity, but clearly not meeting the above criteria. The problem is, how is it possible to develop solidarity and the attendant mutuality of trust where these conditions do not obtain—or is it possible at all?

As a first approach to an answer it may be said that the family is the "primordial" solitary unit of all human societies. Indeed, in the most primitive, kinship, which includes much more than the nuclear family, is the mode of organization of *all* solidarity. Furthermore, it is within these units that all the principal human needs are met. In a modern society this can be true only for the small child. For him "dependency" in the most diffuse sense is more highly concentrated in his relations within this small unit than in any other previous social conditions—a unit which we have seen is more sharply distinguished from others, both of kinship and of nonkinship constitution. As the child matures he develops a variety of roles outside his family. First, perhaps, come neighborhood play groups, then participation in formal education in the school with, concurrently, a new order of relation to age-peers—in the elementary school period virtually confined to the same sex, later increasingly involving the opposite sex. Then more or less well coordinated in time comes emergence into the adult responsibilities of occupational roles and of marriage. The latter usually eventuates in parenthood.

One aspect of the process is that from total and intense dependency on the family of orientation the child becomes increasingly independent from *that* nuclear family, and he continues to play a wide range of nonfamilial roles in his later life. Indeed his capacity to do so successfully is one of the two principal indices of the success of the socialization function in the family of orientation. But the other dramatic aspect is the switchover from family of orientation to the new family of procreation through marriage. The intensity of its emotional significance is attested by the pattern of romantic love on the one hand and the deep concern for having children on the other—both of which are in important part motivated by residues of childhood socialization experience.

Finally, let me emphasize again that the modern family has been deprived of a whole range of its historic functions, particularly those of economic production, but also others. It has become not only a structurally differentiated but a functionally specialized agency. What then can be said about the significance of these remaining specialized functions, not only for the personalities of the individual members but for the wider society?

I suggested above that solidarity was one of four principal conditions of the functioning of a social system. The other three may be said to be economic productivity, political effectiveness, not only for the society as a whole but also for its important collectively organized subsystems, and the integrity of institutionalization of its value commitments. Comparison with one or more of these three may yield suggestions of the significance of what is gained by individuals in their families of orientation and, as it were, "stored" in those of procreation.

The comparison may seem farfetched, but I suggest quite seriously that the grounding of the value of money in "real assets" and its most elementary form in metal coinage are the "primordial" bases of productivity in a sense parallel to that in which family solidarity is the primordial basis of social solidarity generally, "guaranteed" by the personal security of the individual. It is the groundwork on which the possibility of mutual trust in ramified systems of associative relationships—and hence openness to mutual influence—is built in a complex society. Furthermore, because of the irreducible element of ascription on the parent-child relationship, this significance of family solidarity comes to focus in that of the marriage relationship. One of the striking features of modern marriage is, of course, its increasingly voluntary character. This is the product of a long evolution from maximally prescriptive marriages in kinship terms, through marriages arranged by parents and other kin. It is the prototypical, fully unfettered personal commitment to a merging of interests, fortunes, and responsibilities. It is, however, not a simple contract for the mutual furtherance of specific interests, but a diffuse merging, with understood differentiation of function, "for better, for worse, for richer, for poorer," etc. This establishes a certain presumption, that persons capable of honestly undertaking such a commitment of mutual loyalty, including the attendant responsibilities of parenthood, may be regarded as generally trustworthy persons.

It is this generalization of the presumption of trustworthiness which seems to me to be the most crucial societal asset grounded in the solidarity of the family. To help in understanding how this can work it may be recalled that in the parallel context the value of money is grounded in the economic utility, first of real assets generally, then of its metal "base." I suggest that the solidarity of marriage is parallel to the utility of gold—perhaps a not unfamiliar figure of speech. But money as medium of exchange is not a real asset in the present sense: it has no "commodity value." It is a means of acquiring real assets and in turn can itself be acquired by selling them, but as the medium it cannot be consumed. Its significance lies in the possibility of a kind of pooling of the resources of the exchanging system. This involves increased risk for units who put some of their resources into monetary form—as they must if such a system is to operate. But if the value of the medium is secure, the units taken severally and the system as a whole gain enormously in productive potential, especially when not only finished goods and services but the factors of production become marketable.

The indispensable condition of security of the value of the monetary medium cannot, however, rest only on the intrinsic commodity value of its metallic base. It must rest just as much on confidence in exchangeability for real assets, including the availability of such assets in the system—hence the general level of productivity of the system.

The analogue of money as a measure of utility and medium of economic exchange in the field of social solidarity is what, in a technical sense, I have called influence [4]. By this I mean generalized capacity to persuade, through giving "good reasons" why the object of influence should believe or do something in "his own interest." The outcome of successful use of influence in this sense is an increased level of consensus or solidarity in the system to which both belong—though of course the relation to third parties remains problematical.

Persuasion may be carried out by "intrinsic means," e.g., direct information of commitment of intentions to specific action. This is analogous to the exchange of real assets through barter. What I mean by influence goes beyond this to persuade and thereby mobilize commitments, power of control of resources, through a generalized symbolic medium. This consists essentially in the "reputation" of the user of influence for a combination of integrity in commitment to the values presumptively shared with the object of influence, ability to help mobilize the necessary resources, and competence in implementing any action implications of the achieved consensus. Thus to take an example which is very familiar, physicians very generally use influence to get the consent of patients or their families to recommended regimes of treatment. Information alone would not do because so frequently the layman is not competent to evaluate technical information even if it is given to him. He must *trust* both the physician's competence and his integrity. Without the institutionalization of this truth, the presumption that a physician is *trustworthy*, the effectiveness of health care in our complex society would be very much lower than it is. This, however, is only one of many examples which could be adduced. The necessity for influence to bridge the gap between the responsibilities taken by political leadership and the competence of their constituents to evaluate the issues by themselves is certainly one of the most striking instances. The assassination of President Kennedy brought out with special vividness the extent to which not only Americans but much of the world depended on his leadership and was in fact accessible to his influence—however severe the limits to which it was subject, e.g., to Congress. This influence is, in turn, a function on the one hand of the great office of the American Presidency and on the other of the personality of the incumbent.

If, then, influence can be considered to be a generalized medium parallel to money—and to political power—it would be reasonable to believe that on the one hand its value is grounded in the "gold" of family solidarity, while on the other hand it depends on the capacity of the relevant social system or systems to achieve, maintain, and extend its solidarity, expressed above all in its capacity to achieve consensus in matters involving actual and potential conflict of interest. Clearly, trusting others, especially those with whom one does not have a prior diffuse relation of solidarity, involves risk, just as leaving one's economic assets in banks rather than in gold involves risk. The prevalence of anxiety over the risks of trust is eloquent testimony to this. Thus there is a vocal minority who consider all medical practitioners to be no better than pious frauds who simply exploit the helplessness and gullibility of their patients. Others, or many of the same people, consider all politicians to be simple parasites, who are promoting their personal interests at the expense of the public. Finally, the seriousness of basic mistrust in international affairs, especially where ideological conflicts are involved, scarcely needs further comment.

Furthermore, there are many different levels of differentiation of influence systems, which can be analyzed as parallel to that of monetary systems extending from simple market exchange, through the marketability as noted of the factors of production, notably labor and capital, to complex systems involving elaborate forms of banking and credit. The parallel to simple markets for consumers' goods lies in the use of influence to persuade people to make decisions and commitments which are immediately within their capacities or spheres of freedom of action to make. Thus a physician may use his influence to persuade a patient to accept a recommended course of treatment though at the sacrifice of time, money, and other things, including the assumption of risks.

It is a much further step in differentiation to establish systems where the factors involved in enhancing the solidarity of a system are themselves mobilized by the use of influence. A major type of example would seem to be those elements of educational processes which are essentially optional in the system in question. Thus in order to be influential, the physician must have been properly trained. We tend, in evaluating professional training, to emphasize the factor of competence, but it would seem that reputation for integrity is no less important, and indeed access to facilities—i.e., through membership in the staff of a first-rate hospital—would not be neglected. Hence from this point of view medical education may be regarded in part as an "influence-producing industry," in that it produces a class of professional people who have a far higher capacity than would otherwise be the case to persuade people to accept good health care. The ubiquitous resistances to such acceptance should make it clear that this is by no means to be taken for granted.

The analogy to credit in influence systems raises problems of sufficient complexity so that within the limits of this brief paper, it is probably best not to enter into them. One more general point about such systems does, however, need to be made. This is that the basic organizational form of influence systems is the voluntary association. This is not, however, a matter of presence or absence, but of a component in all relational systems with a collective significance. Influence, however, is a medium of persuasion and a person is not in the relevant sense genuinely persuaded unless he is entirely free to reject the influence. Intermixture with economic inducements, with explicit or implied coercive threats, or even appeal to prior commitments is not "pure" persuasion. Generally speaking, the voluntary association is the relational nexus within which there can be said to be a presumption of the achievability of consensus. It will be limited on the one hand by boundaries of membership, which may be more or less formalized, and on the other by boundaries of relevant content—thus consensus with one's physician is relevant within the sphere of health, but not, for example, within the sphere of political opinion.

In the light of these considerations, which may seem to digress a long way from the traditional interests of family sociology, let us now come back to the contemporary family. First, this functional context may throw some light on the significance of some of the trends of development of that family. My suggestion here is that it is to be expected that the family would, as the foundation of the solidarity-influence system, itself develop progressively in the direction of the voluntary association. In the aspect of marriage this is very clear indeed—namely, the trend to make marriage as nearly as possible a purely personal and voluntary relationship. This has gone to the point where the depth of commitment is considered to a high degree to be a function of its voluntary character. More problematical, but highly significant, is the tendency to bring children into the status of members of a voluntary association much earlier and more extensively than before. Of course there is an inherent limitation to this trend in that infants cannot rationally "choose" their parents, but this is clearly a major trend in the American family. Like other such trends it has undoubtedly had its excesses, and surely its limits are not yet clearly defined, but that it is a fundamental trend can scarcely be doubted. Perhaps the most important keynote is that by the isolation of the marriage pair from "structural supports" of more or less ascribed character, children are put in a position of having to trust their parents to an extremely high degree. The corollary is that parents will be expected to reciprocate this trust to an increasing degree, hence to trust children as far as possible as responsible members of the family association.

In this connection it is particularly important to note that what I call trust is *not* to be identified with moral commitment. Common values are certainly essential to the solidarity of any social system, but as *one* factor, not as its totality. Most problems of trust in the present sense arise at a different level where, presuming common values, the questions concern action within the sphere of autonomous personal responsibility. On the part of many parents, and more generally the "view-with-alarm" school of thought on the problems of contemporary youth, the tendency is to confuse the two, and to treat as essentially a moral problem what should be one of trust in the present sense. On the part of young people trained in independence, defining problems as moral tends to activate anxiety about the basic consensus—the complaint is, "Don't you trust me?"

A second major set of considerations emerges. This is that while the family is the primary locus of most elementary instrumental learning for children, e.g., walking and talking, and is for both children and adults an essential agency for meeting their biological and other needs, e.g., food, sleep, relaxation, etc., its most crucial functions lie in the area of solidarity. In socialization it is above all the agency for establishing cathexes and identification, for integration into the series of *social* systems in which the child will function as an adult. Above all, perhaps, it is the primary agency for developing his capacity to integrate with others, to trust and be trusted, to exercise influence, and to accept legitimate influence. Here, of course, two axes are essential. One is the balance of trust over distrust, the "intensity" component. The other is the component of generalization. This is the capacity to enter into solitary relations over a *range,* both of associative partners and of subject-matter areas. In view of the increasing pluralism of our type of society, this is a particularly critical factor. It has become essential for the responsible citizen to be able to balance a variety of complex contexts of obligation and expectation, to be ready to enter into many, but not arbitrarily to sacrifice the interests of some to others. My suggestion would be that the family type which approaches the pattern of voluntary association is the best instrument for laying the foundations of this capacity—though it must be supplemented by other agencies. For the adult the combination of marriage and parenthood in such a family type provides a more or less optimal basis for maintaining the motivational foundations of this more generalized capacity. In this connection socialization and adult participation are above all related in that the capacity to become a good spouse and parent is the underlying capacity for effective participation generally in solitary relations.

Finally, a third inference may be drawn. The "intrinsic utility" of gold is connected with certain features of its sheer physical stability. Its problematical feature is not this but its scarcity. The "gold" of solidarity, however, seems to be an intrinsically unstable entity. Its value depends on its being scarce in the sense that persons who disperse their deepest interpersonal loyalties too widely, e.g., through incapacity to commit them adequately to their marriages and their own children, thereby on the whole lessen their capacity for trust in more generalized and impersonal contexts. But the balances in the personality system, and the meshing of the several commitments in the family, seem to be inherently complex and precarious. This seems to be the most fundamental reason why, once socialized, the typical individual is not finished with family problems, but positively *needs* to marry and to have children.

It would seem to follow that in so far as families are placed under strain, their tendencies to breakdown and various social pathologies should be expected to be conspicuous. Hence I have long felt that what underlay the high divorce rates of our society was not, as so commonly alleged, the decline in the importance of marriage, people's "indifference" to it, but exactly the reverse [5]. Divorce is an index of the severity of the burden placed on the marriage relationship in modern society, and back of that, of the importance of its functions. It is not correct to treat it in any simple sense as a symptom of "decline," except the decline of older patterns of social organization which in any case could not be fitted in with the other principal features of modern society. Essentially the same can be said of failures in the socialization of children, which, of course, are many. Modern child training is far more difficult and demanding on the parents but also on the children themselves than before. In this matter one should not be misled by economic affluence and the like. The hard physical work of a traditional farm boy is not nearly as difficult psychologically as the demands of secondary and higher education and adjustment to peers where the relationship patterns are freely responsible and not ascribed. Whether there is a larger proportion of serious breakdowns than in earlier times is exceedingly difficult to judge—the very anxiety generated by the present difficulties certainly predisposes to the expectation of failure. But that a substantial proportion should be expected is almost in the nature of the relation of the family to the general society of which it is such an essential part.

I was asked to write about the normal American family. In doing so, however, one is eventually led to some consideration of its strains and pathologies. In conclusion, especially since this is a group predominantly of social workers, it seems appropriate to say a few words about that group in which the strains and difficulties of the modern family situation, as in other respects, are most highly concentrated, namely, those who stand lowest on the familiar scales of socioeconomic status, as by family income, education, job level, housing, and type of neighborhood.

Both with respect to the family and in other respects the trends of development of modern society have led to a concentration of certain problems in this lowest group, and by differentiation to a removal or weakening of the structural supports of the kind which, for example, have been more characteristic of the lower statuses in peasant societies— though the tendency to romanticize rural life should not lead one to overlook the reality of many noxious "rural slums." From a middle-class perspective absolute levels of deprivation stand out very prominently, but sociologically it seems more important to emphasize *relative* deprivation. By this I mean that the general trend of development in our society has included a massive upgrading of standards in many respects and the inclusion of much higher proportions of the population in the

groups enjoying the higher standards. Education and the general standard of living are perhaps the most conspicuous contexts, but it is also
important that the proportion of the labor force in unskilled occupations
has declined greatly.

The great source of difficulty is, of course, that in spite of many
improved welfare arrangements, in a society where mobility and hence
competition for preferment are so conspicuous, it has not yet proved
possible to prevent a very substantial residual group from failing to
meet what, however vaguely, must be defined as the minimum generally acceptable standards. To a degree and in certain respects it is
legitimate to treat these cases as "failures" at the individual level, but
it is surely much more a failure of the society in that though some
persons brought up in the lowest conditions succeed in lifting themselves out of them, those set in them by and large are certainly severely
handicapped in a wide variety of ways.

It is well known what a wide variety of "social problems" is concentrated in this group: poverty itself; substandard housing; educational
retardation and early "dropout"; juvenile delinquency; alcoholism; illness, both physical and mental; broken families; and others. It is clearly
a vicious circle which, like the high divorce rates more generally, is in
important part a consequence of the generally rapid process of upgrading. Thus, to take one example, the very rise in general educational
standards makes the position of the relatively handicapped—whether by
low IQ, lack of family support, or other factors—relatively *more* difficult. I suggest that this is a major factor in juvenile delinquency.

It is a healthy sign that there are recent indications of increased
concern over this situation as a national problem, a concern apparently
brought to focus primarily by two interconnected developments, namely,
the new phase of the struggle of the Negro for equality and the chronic
unemployment connected with automation, even in an economy which
is developing at a relatively normal rate.

Whatever the residue of a genuine "caste" system in the South,
which is certainly rapidly breaking up, on the national level it has long
been clear that basically the race problem is a *class* problem, but in a
dual respect. The more obvious one is that the Negro, especially in
urban society, has in fact been predominantly in lower-class status, and
that in so far as there is any empirical truth in his imputed character-

istics, these have been the characteristics shared with other lower-class groups. Indeed in study after study, for example, of such "pathological" behavior as delinquency, it has turned out that if class is controlled sufficiently rigorously the differences by race are negligible.

The second primary aspect, however, is that the Negro has become a, if not the, primary *symbol* of lower-class status. The new phase of the protest movement testifies that he himself is coming to be much less willing to accept this imputation, but it is this symbolic status which is at the core of the whole resistance to granting equal status. Furthermore the resistance centers in the white groups who feel insecure in their own status. The nonrational "reasoning," which must be interpreted in psychoanalytic terms, is to the effect that "if to be lower class is to be black, since I am white there is no danger of *my* falling into that status." Acceptance of the Negro in basically equal status, thus, would remove an important symbolic support to the security of the least secure white elements. The latter are presumably concentrated near the margin of lower-class status, but need not be found only there [6].

It has recently been much publicized that the Negro has double the rate of unemployment of the white labor force, which is a dramatic confirmation of this status since it is in these lower groups generally that unemployment is concentrated.

There is no space to discuss this general situation further. I would like only to point out the relevance of my main analysis to this context. It may, that is, be reasonably supposed that a major factor in the vicious circle to which the lower class, white and Negro alike, is subject lies in the field of the relations between the family and the solidarity and influence systems with which it articulates. My essential point is that this is a two-way and not a one-way relation. By nearly every criterion "family disorganization" is particularly prevalent in the lower class. Not only is this one principal source of the other social problems in that group, but in another sense it is not an isolated phenomenon. It is in part a consequence of the low input to lower-class families of influence in the special form of "social acceptance": from the point of view of the higher groups they are "the wrong kind of people."

Though it is not possible to mobilize the relevant evidence here, I think it is adequate to support the proposition that broadly the lower class, including its Negro component, is not characterized by basically different value commitments from those of the higher groups. It is true that members of the lower class are economically disadvantaged. Perhaps their least serious handicap lies in the field of political power since both the ballot and power through trade unions is available to them, though very incompletely mobilized.

My own view, however, is that the critical problem of the status of the lower class is social acceptance. From any points of view accessible to social policy, it seems to me that in particular it is futile to expect that by exhortation lower-class families will be motivated to pull themselves together. Indeed, I am of the opinion that economic subsidies will not be effective unless they are accompanied by social support on a sufficient scale. The cure for the ills of the lower-class family is a massive input of the very social medium for which the higher-class (not upper-class) family is the primary base in our society in one major set of respects—influence in the form of social acceptance.

The essential goal of any such policies would be to break down group identifications which are interpreted directly, or indirectly as by the criterion of race, as lower class in the invidious residual sense. The neighborhood, the school, and the church are probably the crucial empirical areas for the important reason that the more limited the social participation, the more it is confined to the more immediately personal concerns of the family. Thus increased income would be likely to be important only so far as it enables families to break away from lower-class identifications, e.g., by neighborhood.

It would be expected that improvement in the solidarity of families at the lowest socioeconomic levels would be perhaps the most sensitive index to the success of such social policies. There must always be a bottom of any social scale with a hierarchical aspect, and an achievement-oriented society must be partly hierarchical. But this does not mean that the "outside" status of the present lower class is inevitable. I regard this as perhaps the most important single internal challenge to American society today.

References

1. Another important set of facts concerns the very large proportion of single-family dwellings in this country, and within this, the high proportion of owner occupancy.

2. The psychoanalytic tendency has been to "individualize" these relations by treating a child's relation to each of the other members one at a time —his mother, his father, his rivalry with a particular sibling, etc. More recently, however, there has emerged, particularly in the work of Theodore Lidz and his associates, a tendency to treat the family as a system in such a way that both illness and normality are conceived to be a function of the impact of the system as a whole—not of particular members in isolation—on the individual.

3. Erik Erikson has, in his *Childhood and Society,* given an especially clear formulation of this point in his discussion of the importance of what he calls "basic trust" and its relation to personality development.

4. Cf. Talcott Parsons, "On the Concept of Influence," *Public Opinion Quarterly,* Spring, 1963.

5. To take an analogy which I think is appropriate, the distressing toll of highway accidents is an index of the positive importance, and even, to a degree, of the successful ordering, of vehicular traffic. There is one way to abolish such accidents, namely, to eliminate motor vehicles. Similarly, modern divorce could be quite certainly eliminated if we went back to a primitive kinship system. But we are not, in either case, ready to pay the cost.

6. It is important to note that I do not identify lower and "working" class here. The solid upper-working-class groups, especially in the more skilled trades, seem to be pretty definitely included in the main national community in a sense in which the lower are not.

THE FORCES OF CHANGE

Moderator: Leo Lowenthal

Dr. Lowenthal has published many works related to the sociology of literature and popular culture, including Literature, Popular Culture and Society. Before joining the University of California faculty, he was associated with the Voice of America, Columbia University, and the Center for Advanced Study in the Behavioral Sciences at Stanford, California.

Panel Members: Ping-ti Ho, Herma Hill Kay, Talcott Parsons

Dr. Lowenthal We have heard from Professor Kay about the marital fate which shattered the male utopia of the eighteenth and nineteenth centuries. We were completely disappointed by Professor Ho in destroying the myth of the patriarchal figure in the Chinese family; it turns out that the mother and wife were the real masters and tyrants, to use his own term. To heap injury upon insult, Professor Parsons told us that the women are even living longer than the men. I think that these three papers have enormous intellectual import.

I was very glad to note in Professor Kay's paper that for once the state of Mississippi has contributed to progress, although it was in the thirties of the nineteenth century. Also, I think that Professor Ho contributed to easing us slightly into accepting the recognition of Mainland China by Charles de Gaulle.

Prof. Kay I think Professor Parsons and I agreed with each other quite a bit in our presentations, and I would like to ask whether he would comment further on the way in which the social structure and change in the family has been taking place in the American social system.

Prof. Parsons I believe profoundly in the importance of the family system, and I furthermore don't think it always follows, but at times it leads, social change. I was particularly interested in Mrs. Kay's point of the beginning emergence of a legal status of the family as a whole, which is not a legal status of any particular member or any one relationship between dyads. This is certainly a major trend in society.

It is a very conspicuous development in psychiatric thinking that instead of considering the patient as an individual, there is a marked tendency to see that patient as a member of a family, whose problems are all intertwined with one another. Not infrequently the main source of the trouble is somebody who is not defined as sick, so I think this is very much in line with these important developments.

I would like to ask Professor Ho how he feels about the ancient association, which is as old as human history, between connubium and commensality. If I understood him correctly, he suggested that Chinese society was dividing them, and it might stick that people who lived together in the connubium of husband and wife and certainly in some sort of residential relation to their children in the early stages would cease to share meals and do so permanently.

I take it that connubium and commensality are not the problem, the essentials of which would be this: there is a certain sense in which the essential aspect of the family is what we might call sharing, the sharing of the common household as the residual refuge from strain and tension, which is above all associated with the place where one sleeps, as sleep is our refuge from the strains of the waking life in certain respects. There is a very intimate psychological association between this complex and that of the sharing of food and the social context of the food function. Not only is this so for the family but it is also for a certain character of relations to nonfamily members; for example, in America the invitation to share a meal in a family home is a very strong symbolization of friendship and solidarity.

I take it in Communist China one cannot show one's friendship with one's friends by inviting them to a meal. I don't know whether you are allowed to invite them to your table in the common mess or whether seats are assigned and people may not change the seating arrangements, but you see my general point.

Prof. Ho As a student of history I may have an advantage of being somewhat less likely to be disturbed by the occurrence of a probably transient and at least nonpermanent phenomenon. For one thing, I am not so sure whether the communes in Communist China are still going strong, and, of course, during the past few years, as far as we know, the food situation was bad and the family's monthly ration was so small that even if the Chinese still retained their old virtue of hospitality, they could hardly afford to be hospitable anymore. On the other hand, I learn from my own relatives, who all happen to be members of the professional class and as such are treated as a privileged class in a by and large underprivileged nation or society, that they still invite their friends for dinner. Even if they have to forego some meals and save up enough for a treat for a friend, they can still do that.

In a society such as that on the Chinese mainland, the professional people have one advantage which has almost entirely disappeared here: they still can afford to have servants even though about 80 per cent of the Chinese are in the working force, living in communes. This appeared true up to late 1960, but since then we have learned very little about the communes except that perhaps the family in the narrow sense is still there and working surprisingly well under circumstances so much more difficult than we find here. I think that any information we can receive from qualified observers of China is going to be extremely valuable.

Some sixteen or eighteen months ago a highly trained Western Chinese intellectual, who was born and brought up in Vancouver, revisited Canada because his octogenarian father was ill, and it was his holy filial duty to ask for a special permit to come back to this continent to pay his father his respects and to offer him comfort. His wife accompanied him, a highly educated young Chinese lady, daughter of a former vice-president of the Bank of China in Shanghai. Among the various true stories they told us, I was most touched by one in connection with food rationing. As intellectual workers, they had a somewhat larger ration than the ordinary Chinese, but still they had to save practically a whole month's meat coupons to treat themselves to a good meat meal. On such an occasion their three teen-age children refused to tackle the meat for several minutes. They asked their parents to eat their meat first; of course, the parents had to lead the way. After a while the children refused to eat more than what they believed to be their due share. It took the parents quite a time to explain to them that they, as adults, do not need as much protein as the fast-growing teen-ager. Only after hearing this did they begin to eat more than their shares.

I think whatever is the true intention of the Chinese Communist state, and whatever its power, the character of the Chinese nation will probably continue. No matter how ruthless a state is, it depends on a general and public acquiescence, and if there is a law that affects the family which runs counter to human nature, I have very little doubt as an historian that it would not work and that it would be resisted.

Dr. Lowenthal I have been asked two questions which are almost the reverse of each other: "China has always felt itself to be the center of the world and thus has remained more withdrawn and self-contained than any other advanced civilization. Certainly throughout a long history their concept of social institutions has been advanced. Do you think the Chinese post-1949 concept of the family institution will spread to Western civilization?"

The other question is: "Has there been time and sufficient so-called progress in China to determine the influence of Western so-called cultural activities, such as jazz, night life, etc., on Chinese families? As has been intimated about Japan, has this helped to break down family relationships and parental authority or respect and caused a decrease in ancestral worship? In other words, have the Western cultural activities connected with mass media had a disruptive influence on the traditional Chinese concepts?"

Prof. Ho I think the Chinese usually believe themselves to be situated in the center of the world, hence the expression "middle kingdom"; but this does not mean that China has throughout her long centuries been little affected by the outside world. The more I study Chinese history the more I think that the relations between China and the outside world are to be explored and systematically studied, but I don't think that China was ever truly isolated from the rest of the world. Whether the much weakened and simplified Chinese family system spread to the West I cannot answer very definitely, but I think it is not merely a coincidence that Mrs. Kay and myself in our papers concluded on exactly the same words, namely "the family will survive." In other words, the difference between the present Chinese family and our own family system is not one of kind but only one of degree.

The Peking regime's onslaught on the family and its use of force to compel a certain number of young Chinese to criticize, expose, and condemn their family members during a period of both internal and international tension may not be representative at all, but it is largely because of the state's excessive action against the family during the early fifties that there is a widespread impression that the Chinese family is going to become or has become weakened. Actually I found very little difference between the much reduced functions of the Chinese family and the families of the West.

Concerning mass media, which have long become standard parts of our society, these are luxuries in China. When a rural commune can own a radio set, it usually takes a great deal of pride in this. On the other hand, we do know that there has been a mass educational campaign against certain feudalistic aspects of the Chinese family, such as the doctrine of filial duty.

Have the entertainment aspects of radio, dance music, and so on contributed to a lessening of respect and family cohesion?

I would say rather on the contrary, because among peasant families that belong to the commune, the evening hours are usually the best family hours since the parents and children all spend them together. There is a great deal of love and affection, as Dr. Lazure reports. Therefore I don't think that the entertainment aspects of mass media in any way really weaken the Chinese family.

On the contrary, I would like to cite the experience of a French sinologist. He and his Chinese wife lived for six months in 1958–1959 in North China where the rural communes had just been set up. From talking to a number of the commune housewives, his wife learned that they used to quarrel a great deal with their husbands because of the pressures of life and the daily chores. After the setting up of the commune dining halls, nurseries, etc., the wives confessed that their relations with their husbands had improved. In other words, they felt much less tense and tired in the evening and could afford to be better tempered.

From the Floor Increasingly, nonfamily organizations are being described in terms traditionally associated with the family, as, for instance, the corporation as a family. Perhaps the decline of the family as a legal, socioeconomic unit can be related to the growth of the social and emotional ties of the corporation, the country club, and so on, and thus paradoxically, while the family is being narrowed, in a larger sense its values and components are being extended to the community at large. For instance, President Kennedy's death was regarded by many as a personal family tie loss. Would Professor Parsons discuss this?

Prof. Parsons First, may I raise a question about the word "decline" used in this context. I think there is often confusion on this point. I do not regard differentiation as synonymous with decline. Historically one of the very critical events of the development of modern industry in its early phases was the separation of the productive unit from the household. In traditional agriculture they are fused together as one unit. In the farm family, the household is a producer of agricultural commodities, and also a residential consumer household in our urban centers. When we use the word "family" to designate the stage before differentiation has taken place, as in the farm family, and use the same word to designate one of the two outcomes of the process of differentiation, we must say, "Of course, the family has lost its function." There is a certain logical absurdity in this. Anything that lives has certain functions, even though they may have declined. I think that the question of whether or not the family has declined in the functional sense of not doing its job must be judged in the context of its contemporary relation to other things because it is often exceedingly desirable that differentiations of this sort be made.

The extension, symbolism, and analogies of the family is a very old concept. Priests of the Roman Catholic Church are called Father; in all branches of Christianity we are called children of God, the Father; members of religious orders are brothers and sisters. There is certainly nothing new about the use of family symbolism in a nonfamilial context. It may well be, however, that there are certain new usages, and it is very common to hear "Oh, it is all in the family" or "We're all one big family" as an assertion of solidarity and belonging together. This is a kind of tribute to the family.

Dr. Lowenthal Would Professor Kay elaborate upon the family court and the function it has taken over from the family itself, and touch briefly on or predict the impact of our changing welfare laws upon the family? Has there been a serious trend toward so-called voluntary abandonment, and what has been the impact on the family and the law?

Prof. Kay To speak first about the family court, this is an idea which, as I said, has been suggested primarily by people who work with the juvenile courts in this country. The only family court that is now functioning in the exclusive sense of the word is the Family Court of Toledo, Ohio, of which Judge Alexander is and has been the guiding spirit for some years.

The idea of the family court is not so much to take over functions that the family no longer performs but to create in one court, with one judge and one staff of experts, a simple file of information about families that come into a court to have problems solved. For example, in California, juvenile matters are handled in the Juvenile Court Department, divorce matters in the Superior Court Department, and adoption and child-custody matters may be cited without relation to either of these other two, even if the families concerned have been previously before the court. The idea of the family court is to build up one jurisdiction to solve, handle, or treat all these problems as a unit, and we have already in California, I think, a movement toward this kind of establishment. We have not yet proposed that it be integrated with the juvenile court since these develop separately; we like to emphasize the other aspects first, and perhaps later on the two can come together.

As to the other idea about the impact of the social welfare legislation on family law, I should like to refer to one article on this point that was written some years ago on the impact of social welfare legislation on family law. The impact, I think, has been primarily aimed at the existing family laws as to support and the duties of parents to children and to each other.

We have a situation in which the Civil Code states absolutely that the stepfather is not liable for the support of his stepchildren. Yet in the Welfare and Institutions Code there is a provision that in calculating the allowance in Aid to Needy Children one must take into account not only the income of the stepfather who is living in the home, but also the income of a man who is "performing the functions of a spouse to a woman, whether he is married to her or not." So we are assessing not only a stepfather's obligations but those of a lover as well. This has an interplay on family-law structure.

In several cases where the interplay has been discussed, the court has said, "We try to read the Code as a whole and harmonize it as much as possible." What is really meant is that the Social Welfare Department has administered its own, without considering the Civil Code.

From the Floor   "Is there a possible link between the mother fulfilling her child-rearing responsibilities and leaving for work too soon for the child to assume the responsibility of independence and freedom?"

Prof. Parsons   I strongly emphasized that the tendency is for the family cycle to become increasingly differentiated. This question concerns a matter of timing which is always complicated and often difficult in the particular case.

At just what age can children spare the mother's not quite undivided (most married women have husbands) attention? They always require some attention, but when do they need major attention? The child is in school a large part of the day. I am inclined to think that secondary school, which includes afternoon activities after class, is a common dividing line. Also there are possibilities, which appear to be increasing, in part-time work. I was in a meeting concerning personnel associated with mental health. Two of the people at the meeting spoke about the serious shortages of nurses and teachers. Both said that by far the best reserve pool is trained married women who have been out of the labor force but who can be induced to come back.

In part-time work careful attempts are made to reconcile it with family responsibility, but this is a very complicated area and much more needs to be done in it. It is a little like the abruptness of retirement: one day you have a full-time job, the next no job at all. There has been a tendency to define any employment as either full employment or not employment at all, which ignores the complicated problems of fitting together different kinds of obligations of different classes of people. There is a slow trend to improve the fit, and to open more and more opportunities for something other than either-or, but I wouldn't doubt that a good many married women do go back into the labor force too early. I doubt whether it is the great majority.

From the Floor   In a divorce in California, the decision with reference to children is overwhelmingly in favor of the woman. Why is there this discrimination? Would it not be better under the circumstances to relocate the children to a new and neutral home to avoid bitterness and confusion?

Prof. Kay   I think there should be justice. The law of child custody starts with the presumption that neither parent has the paramount right to custody. This is a change from the common-law attitude, where the father definitely had the sole right to custody after divorce. One point to be made is that the California statutes give a preference to the mother if the child is of tender years, and the preference is given to the father if the child is of an age to be prepared for higher education or training in business and labor. What this means in practice is that initially children who are very young remain with the mother. Whether or not this is fair or unfair to fathers has been the subject of much discussion and litigation in California. One point to be made is that normally one expects a woman to stay at home more than a man, although in view of Professor Parsons' statistics of 50 per cent of married women now working outside the home, perhaps our assumption is no longer warranted. If it isn't, certainly the law should take this into account, but I don't think that you can say that there is an unfair discrimination against fathers in so far as the law is written. Should there be some way to put the child in a neutral home for a while to free him of the bitterness that is attendant to divorce? There have been cases in California where the custody was awarded to the father on the agreement between parents that the child would be placed in the home of his parents. This seemed a reasonable solution, at least in the beginning years when the family was terribly destroyed by bitterness. Yet in an actual case where that happened, the mother complained. She said that her legal rights had been done away with because the child was being taken from her not to be given to her husband, with whom she was on an equal legal basis, but to the husband's parents, who to her were outsiders. The law by its own doctrine had to agree that in fact the custody of the child had in all real sense been given to the grandparents. So I think that an obstacle to our trying to view the child and his needs as an individual for this impartial kind of home is at the moment very much impeded by this legal doctrine, which I, for one, would like to see done away with.

From the Floor   What is the usefulness of family therapy?

Prof. Parsons   I have been interested in this as part of the social organization of therapy. There is no doubt that it is in fact increasing and that there is a growing interest in its potentialities. The opinion among an important group of psychiatrists and other mental health personnel is that it is very important and should have more attention paid to it.

From the Floor   What about the function of the law as a teacher rather than a reflector of our society, in the sense that for so long law in effective terms has been regarded as what the courts will allow or do, or in older terms was a reflection of what the sovereign commanded? Ought not the legal profession to be teaching this society what its nature demands rather than reflecting what it seems to want?

Prof. Kay   I think to a certain extent you can say that legislation can often attempt to serve the function of teaching the society. Of course, lawyers don't have any larger share of truth than anybody else, and I hope that we wouldn't try to set up what is best for a society without the advice and assistance of everybody else concerned with human life. More specifically, it seems to me that you can argue that such laws as those concerning crime, race relations, or basic human dignities can attempt to set a standard that society should attempt to measure up to. The problem is to legislate for a higher degree of morality than the public is willing to accept, and what usually happens is that the law is not lived up to. The great experiment of doing away with alcoholic beverages in this country is a case in point, and I suspect that if we tried to legislatively abolish smoking the results would be the same.

But I don't think this means that the law should not try to aim as high as it can within the realm of what is possible.

From the Floor   Taking into consideration the slim control of the court over the payment of child support by the father, is not the preference to give the young child to the mother an economic discrimination against women rather than an infringement upon the father?

Los Angeles has established a system of decreeing, when the family is under the Aid to Needy Children project or when anybody asks to have it done, that the child-support payments be made payable not to the mother but directly to the court trustee. The court trustee has IBM machines which record the amount, frequency, etc., of the father's payments. If he misses two payments, the IBM machine pulls his card. The court trustee then files a petition with the district attorney's office in Los Angeles County. The district attorney has, I believe, six administrative assistants and four assistant district attorneys working full-time in this program. They bring it into court as a question of civil, not criminal, contempt. The man is cited and appears in court. He may either say, "I don't have the money," or else, "I have paid it directly to the mother," but if he doesn't say either one of those two things he goes to jail. This has proved enormously effective in Los Angeles County. It is much more efficient than the system we have in San Francisco, which requires the mother to go to a lawyer to find the father and bring him into court since she often cannot afford to pay either the child support or the lawyer's fees. I think a partial answer is to enforce the laws we already have.

Dr. Lowenthal I am very happy to see that machines have feelings now.

From the Floor Is it true that in California law a child can be deprived of his liberty without due process of law? I notice over the objections of the grandmother and the parents the child must stay home on the word only of a worker of the Juvenile Department without any trial or court participation.

Prof. Kay The juvenile court law in California was thoroughly reformed in 1961, and I think that now there is much less chance in the law of that happening than there was formerly. One of the chief reforms written into our juvenile court law that has also been reflected, I believe, in New York, is that the lawyers have been put back in the juvenile court process so that the child is entitled to representation by counsel at all stages of the proceedings, and there cannot be an order depriving the parents of custody and control over the child even for a period of as short as ten days without appearing before the juvenile court judge and without a full airing of the pros and cons of the situation. Some of the early juvenile court reforms went too far in taking away all legal and civil rights of the child, but I think we have corrected these abuses in California.

From the Floor   What was the role of concubinage in the family and the kinship system in China before 1949?

Prof. Ho   We must be statistically minded. Rich men who could afford more than one wife must have been at any given time an extremely small example in terms of the total population. The Civil Code of 1931 allowed certain exceptions; that is, if the concubines had already been living and accepted as members of the family, they were allowed to have their rights. But since 1949 concubinage has been strictly prohibited. Now the single sex standard is so strictly enforced that the Chinese might be called a nation of Communist or Confucian Puritans.

From the Floor   Do you think that married women should be encouraged to seek gainful employment when economics is not a necessity, or should they be encouraged to give more direction to family life and the emotional security of their children as well as providing a stable community life through volunteer service?

Prof. Parsons   Fortunately we live in a society where there is a great deal of option for the individuals to make their own decisions and which therefore allows for variation of personality and situation.

I do think that there is an unmistakable trend in the direction of increasing gainful employment of married women, and this unquestionably includes very large numbers where it is not primarily financial pressure. I do not personally deplore this trend, I rather welcome it, but this should not exclude quite other ways of handling the problem of what to do with their freedom.

From the Floor   Professor Kay touched momentarily on property settlements in divorce. It is my understanding that the party suing for divorce is the 'wronged party, and it is customary for the lady to sue the gentleman: therefore the gentleman pays the penalty. I wish you would discuss the relationship of this penalty payment and property settlements which are levied against the gentleman.

Prof. Kay   The law in California changed on that point, I think, around 1952, with the decision of *DeBurgh v. DeBurgh.* The point to be made is that all money can be granted only to a person in whose favor the divorce is granted. Once you have the principle that divorce can be granted in the same action to both parties, it then logically fol-lows that all money can be assessed in favor of both parties, although I have yet to see a case where a wife was ordered to pay alimony. The other problem about property settlement is that there are three grounds for divorce in California, and the community property can be divided unequally. This means that the person who gets the divorce, let's say on the grounds of mental cruelty, can be given theoretically 100 per cent of the community property. Again that almost never happens: the prevailing party is given 51 per cent of the community property to comply with the technical meaning of the statute. It seems to me we should divorce the property settlement from the alimony and view the disposition of property in line with the need of the parties—whether the wife works, is able to support herself, how much money the husband has, etc.—and not who is or who is not at fault.

From the Floor Can you compare the Chinese commune with the Israeli kibbutz, and could you possibly compare the two with the upper-class ideal which has always been to have someone else take care of your children and you enjoy them at your leisure?

Prof. Ho I just learned from Dr. Parsons that in Israel the new experiment seems to have shown signs of being broken up and weak-ened, but in China the upper-class ideals are very attractive. Who likes to take over the daily household chores? If the daily chores can be done by others, then it is all to the good. Apparently that is one of the major reasons why the communes have been tolerated by the mass of people.

Prof. Parsons I didn't want to take too drastic a view of the kibbutz. I am not by any means an expert on it, but I have had some touch with studies that have been made. There has undoubtedly been a trend away from the more rigorous definitions of complete com-munality in which the marriage relationship was restricted to the sharing of a bare room, with an almost blanket prohibition of entertain-ing friends there, and the couple was permitted very limited contact with their children in the period just between the end of the day's work and the communal evening meal in the dining hall. The change has been in the direction of giving more scope to family interests, al-though it is too much to say that it has broken up.

PART TWO

THE SACRIFICE OF FAMILY STRUCTURE

Chairman: C. Easton Rothwell

A nationally known educator, Dr. Rothwell was previously associated with the U.S. Department of State and the United States delegation to the United Nations. Before taking his post with Mills College, Dr. Rothwell was Director of the Hoover Institution and Library at Stanford University.

Having concluded that there was a true value and usefulness of the family in some form today, the symposium moved to a consideration of the important disruptive factors of today. The session opened with a consideration of the delegation of responsibility and authority by parents to the community at large in the modern urban setting. The effects of physical dissolution upon its members were discussed and the contrast between past experience and the present social adaptation analyzed in positive fashion. The psychiatric vantage point then developed the concept of adult immaturity as a major factor in family problems. The panel chiefly concerned itself with determination of whether the changes from traditional family concepts really implied the sacrifice of its structure and brought out the importance of point of view in the analysis of the situation today.

THE SOCIAL CHALLENGE TO PARENTAL AUTHORITY

Neil J. Smelser

Editor of the American Sociological Review, *Dr. Smelser is particularly interested in social change and the relation between personality and social structure and the theory of collective behavior. His latest publications concern these fields of sociology.*

Sociological research in the past few decades has developed a sort of "orthodox" position concerning the fate of the family in modern times. This position originated primarily with the "Chicago school" of the 1920s and 1930s; leading exponents were William Fielding Ogburn, Meyer Nimkoff, and Ernest Burgess. According to this position, the family has experienced a great withering away of functions as a result of the demands placed on it by the urban and industrial way of life.

The typical argument associated with this position usually unfolds in three phases. The first phase involves an image of a "traditional" family (a "farm family" or a "frontier family," perhaps). This image is often romanticized; it is not often documented by historical research. The traditional family is viewed as economically self-sufficient, or at least embedded in a self-sufficient farm or village community. In this phase, the nuclear family was implicated in a network of extended kinship ties, which included cooperative work and perhaps reciprocal exchanges of gifts. Within the nuclear family the division of labor was strictly regulated by age and sex. The father was responsible primarily for work in the fields, the mother in the house and garden. Children became economic assets at a young age, contributing to productive labor on the farm. The father had great authority over his children and was responsible for supervising and training sons in their economic roles. The emotional relations between father and children were those of respect and distance. The formation of new families through marriage was closely regulated by elders. After marriage a young couple retained close ties with the elders, often in common residence; and the old, being venerated, maintained authority in the traditional family.

The second phase of the argument involves some sort of "shock" imparted to this traditional family by the development of a commercial market structure, by the development of industry, or by the development of cities—usually a combination of all three. The immediate effects of this shock were to draw one or more family members into wage labor (separate from the household), thereby destroying the traditional family division of labor; to make the family more mobile socially and geographically; to place the family in an anonymous social environment; and perhaps to destroy the family's economic base further by flooding the market with cheap, mass-produced products that competed with those previously produced domestically.

The third phase of the argument involves an image of the "modern" family that emerges after the shock. The most fundamental of these changes—imposed mainly by the demands for mobility—is the individuation and isolation of the nuclear family. The reasoning is that if the family has to be mobile, it cannot afford to carry its extended kin with it. Thus ties with collateral kin erode; fewer generations live in the same household; newly married couples set up new households and leave the elders behind. Simultaneously the relations between parents and children undergo a vast transformation. The father, who now has to leave the household for employment in a separate establishment, necessarily loses many of the economic-training and supervisory functions he previously enjoyed over his children. Often, it is claimed, this decline in economic authority spreads to a decline in *general* authority. The former relations of distance and respect between father and son now become relations of intimacy, affection, and equality. The mother, often being the only adult in the presence of young children during large parts of the day, becomes the crucial agent in early socialization.

However concentrated the relations between mother and children in the early years, this period is short-lived. The nuclear family in an urban-industrial environment very early loses control of its children to primary school (or even nursery school); by adolescence the child has outside contacts not only with education but also with some parts of the labor market. Furthermore, many children have married and set up a separate household of their own by the age of twenty, and have become even more independent of their parents.

Both scholars and the general public tend to view such trends with apprehension and dismay. The loss of parental control, one hears, threatens the moral fiber of the society. To this loss of authority, one also hears, it is possible to assign much responsibility for social evils such as delinquency, illegitimacy, teen-age drinking, school dropouts, and so on. Behind such claims, one suspects, lies a sort of diffuse fear that as a society we are "losing control" of the dangerous, explosive forces of childhood and raw youth.

Some recent research has begun to challenge this view of the fate of the family in modern times. First-rate scholars such as William J. Goode are questioning—and informing their questions with serious comparative research—the historical validity of the claims of what happens to the family in the urban-industrial setting. Unfortunately, too little of this research concerns the fate of parental authority. Therefore my remarks on this subject will have to be based partly on speculation. Nevertheless, I think it is possible to be more precise in describing the modern trends of parental authority in our society, and in commenting on the social and moral significance of these trends.

Initially I should like to enter a general note of caution about accepting any pronouncement concerning the precipitous decline of parental authority. Such pronouncements are a general feature, indeed a symptom, of periods of all sorts of social change, not merely social decline. The pronouncements, furthermore, are likely to reflect less the real state of affairs—which can be determined only by careful historical and comparative analysis—than the despair of the commentator. I shall illustrate the need for caution by one citation. The most famous observer of our society had this to say about the relations between fathers and sons in America: "The distance which formerly separated a father from his sons has been lessened; and paternal authority, if not destroyed, is at least impaired." Or again, from the same pen: "The relation of father and son becomes more intimate and more affectionate; rules and authority are less talked of." The observer was Alexis de Tocqueville; the time was 1832, which, by many measures, is in the "farm" or "frontier" era of the family we often romanticize today. The danger of myopia is always with us when talking about the modern fate of society and its institutions.

To address the central question now, I think there are four related but distinct trends in modern times with respect to social authority over children and youth. These four trends do not add up to a general decline of parental authority, but to a much more complicated picture.

The first trend is indeed a *relative decline* in some aspects of parental authority. The clearest example of this is the decline in the parents' economic training and control functions. Fathers no longer apprentice their sons to a trade or teach them to run the farm. Mothers instruct their daughters less than formerly in domestic affairs. Educational institutions and training programs on the job have assumed this aspect of parental authority. Another example of the decline is the parents' loss of control over their children's decisions to marry. The arranged marriage is a thing of the past. Control over courtship has tended to pass into the hands of the children themselves, though the parents and peer groups still exercise much informal control.

The second trend is a consolidation, indeed a *relative increase* in other aspects of the authority of the parents. I refer here to parental responsibility during the first two to four years of the child's life. The modern parent probably has more exclusive guardianship—and hence relatively more authority—over children in these years than in the past, when the extended family and the neighborhood figured more prominently in infant care. The modern child, being less surrounded on an everyday basis by uncles, aunts, adult neighbors, and domestic servants, probably relies more exclusively on his parents as authority models than before.

In connection with these two trends, a paradox arises in the arguments of those who complain of a general decline in parental authority. Those who complain clearly do *not* refer to those areas where a decline is most easily observed—namely, control over economic training and courtship. Indeed, scarcely anyone would argue for the restoration of apprenticeship systems or arranged marriages. Rather, the complaint is about the general moral authority of the parents—their ability to mold the basic personality of the child so he will have a respect for authority. Yet the parents' role in this latter regard appears to loom as large as, if not larger than, in the past because of the diminution of really close substitute authority figures in the early years of the child's life. This paradox suggests that the simple complaint of the decline of parental authority is too easy a diagnosis.

The third trend with respect to authority over children and young people in modern times is that more, in an absolute sense, is being demanded of them than ever before. The field of education provides the best example of this. Prior to the development of formal education, the child probably did not receive much training in literacy. Neither in the past nor in the present has the family been known for its contribution to formal education. With the development of educational institutions, however, a new authority—authority to control the acquisition of reading and writing skills—was imposed on the child. This development meant more than that the family was now sharing what it formerly controlled exclusively; it meant that a new *type* of authority was emerging. Indeed, it is possible to speak of a general increase in demands from authorities over the child in modern times.

The fourth trend is that authority over children and young people has become greatly *dispersed*. True, the very early years of the child's life are, as indicated, years of intensified and concentrated relations with the parents, especially the mothers. After that time, however, the child moves into an ever-widening range of authorities of various sorts— earliest perhaps the baby-sitter, then the nursery school teacher, followed by the complex of teachers, den mothers, scoutmasters, camp counselors, church youth group leaders, and peer group leaders. Not only are more skills and roles being demanded of the young, but a greater variety of persons and agencies are doing the demanding.

Taking these four trends together, it would appear that the social challenge to the family in modern times is not so much the *decline* of parental authority as it is the possible *discontinuity* between various types of authority. In the earliest years of the child's life, the main authority lies in the mother's hands. Typically the father is away large parts of the day, returning for only a few of the child's waking hours and for longer periods on the week end. To establish unambiguous spheres of authority and continuity of authority between mother and father under these arrangements is more difficult than under a traditional division of labor.

In later years the problem of discontinuity persists, but changes form. Now the problem becomes the relations between parental and other kinds of authority. As many investigators have suggested, the conflict between the essentially middle-class standards of schoolteachers and the working-class standards of the parents of the majority of pupils poses a serious discontinuity in authority. The same might be said, in varying degree, for the relations between parental authority and the authority of church groups, youth clubs, settlement houses, and so on.

Two other features of recent American history aggravate these threats of discontinuity: (1) Mass immigration. The authority structure of the family of immigrant groups has been discontinuous, in varying degree, with the demands imposed by dominantly native American teachers, employers, and other authorities. (2) Social mobility. As an individual moves either upward or downward from his parents' position in the stratification system, he is likely to experience standards of authority very different from those of his family of origin. We may conclude, then, with the suggestion that as society becomes complex, heterogeneous, and mobile, the main social problem becomes not so much the absolute amount of parental authority but the relations between parental and other kinds of authority.

CATASTROPHES IN PARTNERSHIP:

SEPARATION, DIVORCE, AND WIDOWHOOD

James A. Peterson

In addition to his work in sociology and anthropology, Professor Peterson is in charge of the Ph.D. Training Program in Family Counselling at the University of Southern California. He is the author of numerous studies on marriage and divorce, including Education for Marriage, Toward a Successful Marriage, *and* The Trouble with Women.

The assessment of statistical comparisons on which to base any projection of trends concerning family disruption is extraordinarily difficult. It is true that the divorce rate per 1,000 population in 1959 as compared with that of 1910–1914 has more than doubled, rising from 1.0 to 2.3. But, as we shall see, there is an increased correlation between class position and divorce rates so that the heavy load of divorce is in the lower-class positions [1]. Whether, then, the increase in total divorce represents only the increased use of legal facilities by these classes we do not know. It is possible that a rising divorce rate may represent a more law-abiding population which signifies disruption with legal means, whereas, previously, the same disruption would have been accomplished by separation or desertion.

While the statistics we shall quote may be interpreted to indicate that the family is in such a state that it must search for survival, this inference is certainly not entirely clear. We shall question this thesis repeatedly in this paper.

The divorce rate has been loosely described as being about one divorce to every four or five marriages, but this statistic is in error because it includes all second and subsequent divorces. It was not until Monahan analyzed in detail the changing nature and instability of remarriage that we had any real insight into the meaning of this statistic. In analyzing the detailed marital backgrounds of all couples in Iowa for 1953–1955, he found widely divergent trends for divorce for the various marital states [2]. The divorce rate for all first marriages was 16.6 per hundred; if both partners had been divorced once, the rate doubled to 34.9 per hundred; if both had been divorced twice or more, the rate again doubled to 79.4 per hundred; but if both had been widowed once, the rate was only 9.9, or about half the rate for the first marriages. Monahan indicates that information gathered for other cities generally confirms these findings, which indicate that some 84 per cent of the population persevere in their initial marriage.

The suggestion that American marriages are falling into the pattern of "serial" or "sequential" polygamy is scarcely supported by this analysis. Monahan estimates that 75 per cent of those first divorced remarry, so that only 12 per cent of the population attempts a second marriage, of which one-third fail. Since the total divorce rate has constantly receded from its high point of 4.3 per 1,000 in 1946 to 2.2 in 1960, the trend must be away from divorce in general and thus inferentially away from "sequential" polygamy.

Certain inferences from Goode's calculations regarding income and education support this conclusion. He calculated a proneness to divorce index, by income [3].

Proneness to divorce index, by income
aged 25–44 years, 1950

Income (1949)	Index
$0	199.0
$1–$999	188.6
$1,000–$1,999	134.8
$2,000–$2,999	92.9
$3,000–$3,999	89.2
$4,000 and over	66.7

He also presents a proneness to divorce index, by education [4].

Proneness to divorce index, by education
white (males) aged 25–44 years, 1950

Education	Index
No school	92.7
Grammar school	101.9
Some high school	109.5
High school graduate	95.0
College	86.1
(Not known)	(183.7)

Both indexes indicate that as income and education increase, the divorce rate decreases. Since both income and educational levels are rising, it is possible to project the correlation in the direction of further reduction in divorce totals. It should be noted, however, that for the Negro segment of the population, the relationship is reversed: as education increases, so does proneness to divorce.

Consideration of teen-age marriage is instructive. There is no question that as age for marriage goes down, the dissolution-of-marriage rate goes up. Paul Glick concludes, after an exhaustive analysis of age of marriage, that

They indicate that a large proportion of women with remarriages had married for the first time at a relatively young age . . . for women who first married before they were 18, the proportion remarried was about half again as high as that for women who first married at 18 or 19; in turn, for those who first married at 18 or 19, the proportion remarried was about half again as high as that for women who first married at 20 or 21 [5].

He goes on to point out that for women who were above twenty-one at the time of first marriage, fully nine out of ten had not remarried after thirty years of marriage. Glick feels that these facts point to the "essential stability" of marriages in the United States. While it is a current fad to point to teen-age marriage as a basic contribution to the divorce rate, we wonder if this conclusion does not need refining. All of the careful studies of teen-age marriage show that between 30 and 60 per cent of youthful marriages involved premarital pregnancies. Such marriages are notoriously unstable. Indeed, they may comprise that portion of teen-age marriages that are unstable. If we were to factor out the forced marriages, we might discover that the remainder had rather remarkable adjustment. This, of course, has not been established because no differentiation has yet been made of such marriages by such categories. Our observation here is that the lumping together of such obviously distinct categories impels us to make rather cautious conclusions regarding the relationship of age to marriage.

The remarkable fact really is that the divorce rate is not a great deal higher than it appears to be. When one considers the rapid shifts in structure, function, and role associated with the transition of the family from an extended, patriarchal system to a nuclear, democratic form; the heterogeneity of cultural backgrounds introduced into each marriage in our mobile society; the loss of external support and social control of community and church; the shearing away of major functions such as economic, religious, educational, recreational, and protective functions which previously bonded the family; the ubiquity of a schizoid, idealistic philosophy of relationship that by definition seems to preclude reality testing; and the really enormous emotional demands implicit in the isolated nuclear family—the over-all divorce rate of 18 per cent for first marriages is startlingly low. When one adds such evidence as that recently introduced by Reuben Hill's painstaking research of three family generations that shows the youngest marriages to be the most competent in planning and decision making and most successful in completing projects, we are hard pressed to explain the success of modern marriage.

One does not minimize the importance of the 16.6 per cent divorce figure of Monahan. This represents about one-sixth of the men and women of the nation. If divorce represents for them failure in their affectional lives or permanent parental deprivation for their children, this fact is dysfunctional indeed. The fact is often cited that children of divorced parents are at a disadvantage and have a higher divorce rate than do children from unbroken homes. But while these statistics are accurate, the influence is not completely clear because their failure may be class-linked rather than divorce-linked. Most of these children are soon involved in a new marriage. Seventy-five per cent of those divorced remarry within five years of their divorce. Bernard studied 2,009 cases of remarriage and concludes that the "general success" of these marriages is about the same as that of first marriages. In studying the impact of the remarriage on children of divorce, she summarizes:

> These sources [Bernreuter Personality Inventory and Interviews] seem to indicate little justification for assuming that the experiences of these subjects have damaged them to any marked degree. Suffering there has been —even, no doubt, serious trauma. But the over-all picture is not one of disorganized young men and women. They do not stand out as unusual, seriously maladjusted, or emotionally crippled. The charge that they are damaged would have to be documented by more convincing evidence than has so far been unearthed [6].

Indeed, if we can conclude with Locke, Goode, and Bernard that the majority of second marriages are certainly better unions than the first attempt and on a par with other first marriages, and if the second marriage provides a healthy emotional environment for the child, it is possible to regard the divorces of these individuals as a part of an efficient family system. Goode describes divorce as a "part of the sifting out process" designed to produce a more rewarding and stable family life for society. These studies of successful second marriages may imply a rather radical revision of the punitive legal approach to divorce which may be partially responsible for the trauma of children and for the increasing hostility between the sexes. In this sense there may be considerable cultural lag in the approach of other social institutions to the modern family. It would be ironic indeed if they, in the name of preserving the family, persisted in attitudes and behavior which inhibited the formation of stable family units.

Marriage failure is often operationally defined not only by divorce but also by separation. It is difficult to know how statistics on separation are related to divorce because our census data is taken on a single day. On that day a couple may be separated, but divorced a month later. Yet we know that a large number of men get the "poor man's divorce" and simply move away. Nevertheless, it is instructive to note that in the 1950 Census the ratio of separated men to divorced men was 1 to 2. If any large percentage of the separated represents permanent separation without subsequent divorce or desertion, this adds a substantial increment to the total number of families that fail. In the case of white men, divorce accounts for well over half of marital instability, but among nonwhites divorces account for only about a third. It is possible that the widowed make up a somewhat larger part of the permanently separated group because they do not remarry as rapidly or in as high a proportion as do the divorced. The widowed first marriage lasts twice as long as the divorced marriage, and, after five years, when 75 per cent of the divorced have remarried, only 50 per cent of widowed men and 25 per cent of the widowed women are remarried. But, as we have seen, where they do, their marriages have a higher possibility of success. It is possible, then, that the category of separation may not really be operational in measuring marital instability, for many widowed men and women may simply choose to remain single.

All that we have said does not contradict the fact that divorce and desertion cost a great deal in human suffering. It is painful for society to watch such armies of young people go up the steps to the altar with joy and all too soon walk down the steps of the divorce court with tears and dejection. Even though Nye, Landis, and the Gluecks have good data to show that children in a home of conflict or separation suffer more than those in a divorced home, there is still stigma to divorce for the child which must influence his self-esteem. However, we have no longitudinal studies to determine what final impact divorce makes on male or female identification or anticipation of marriage.

Our scales are still crude and so far used only in cross-sectional studies. The high divorce figure for children of divorce may or may not infer failure in role identification or positive commitment to the responsibilities of marriage. We suspect long-term trauma but we do not know.

We do know that whatever the residual impacts of separation, desertion, and divorce, they could be fewer if we reduced the incidence of family disruption. We cannot arrest the massive dislocations in the contemporary family that result in what Parsons calls the "disorganization in transition," but through consistent family life education we could make young people aware of changing functions and roles so that their expectations would be more congruent with social reality. In my clinic we see dozens of cases in which the individuals demonstrate no capacity to relate meaningfully on responsibility to others. They will drift into and out of many marital unions. A really serious program of premarital counseling would have spotted them as poor marital material.

Certainly some of those who go through multiple divorces project such major intrapsychic disturbances that only psychotherapy can arrest their march from one pair of arms to another, but the descending divorce rate may well represent a tendency to utilize therapeutic resources more extensively. It is true that children of divorce are often destroyed by being made pawns in the bitter postdivorce struggle of their parents, but we also see couples who come to the clinic before their divorce simply to work out ways of protecting their children. Some courts are described as "divorce mills," but others all over the country are experimenting with methods of protecting children and exploring pathways to reconciliation. Nor can we forget the vast body of research studies which are adding more and more insight into the basic causes of marital sorrow. Exciting experiments in family therapy, group therapy with couples, and marital testing all have promise both for insight into family processes and the development of skilled therapeutic intervention. The American family may be struggling for survival, but it is a vigorous struggle, and it is being waged on many fronts. It may very well turn out that our definition of the struggle may be in error—that what we are really about is the birth struggle of a new and vigorous family system.

References

1. Goode, using sample survey data for the national population, calculated the following table:

Proneness to divorce, by income (male)

Income category (annual)	Divorce proneness index
under $500	189
$500–$999	216
$1,000–$1,999	109
$2,000–$2,999	106
$3,000–$3,999	69
$4,000 and over	45

SOURCE: William J. Goode, *After Divorce*, New York, The Free Press of Glencoe, 1956, p. 53.

2. Thomas Monahan, "The Changing Nature and Instability of Re-marriages," *Eugenics Quarterly*, 5(2):73–85, August, 1958.
3. Goode, p. 54.
4. *Ibid.*, p. 54.
5. Paul Glick, *American Families*, New York, John Wiley & Sons, Inc., 1957, pp. 56–58.
6. Jessie Bernard, *Remarriage*, New York, The Dryden Press, Inc., 1956, p. 318.

ADOLESCENT STRUGGLE AS PROTEST

Nathan W. Ackerman

Author of The Psychodynamics of Family Life, *Dr. Ackerman directs the professional program of The Family Institute and also serves as Clinical Director of the Family Mental Health Clinic in New York City. He has made many contributions to the understanding of family interactions.*

In every age, youth draws judgment on the elders, the elders draw judgment on youth. In a sense, each diagnoses the other.

Justice Douglas characterized the role of youth as "his majesty's loyal opposition"—"Youth, like the opposition party in a parliamentary system, has served a powerful role. It has cast doubts on our policies, challenged our inarticulate major premises, put the light on our prejudices, and exposed our inconsistencies. Youth has made each generation indulge in self-examination." Thus, it is the duty of the son to provide a loyal opposition to his father—to challenge his goals, judgments, decisions, and actions. This is the universal pattern of the son's allegiance to his father. The son rebels, but his very rebellion adds to his father's stature and deepens his wisdom.

For each generation, in turn, the adolescent and adult members of the community must come to terms; they must reach some mutually effective accommodation. Each needs the other. Each is responsible to the other. Each diagnoses the attitudes and actions of the other. The interchange of feeling and influence between the adolescent and his adult environment is a circular one. Something of the character, the dynamic quality, and also the distortions of the close human environment leave their mark on the adolescent. But the converse is also true. Something of the inner warp and woof of the adolescent leaves its mark on family and community.

When this delicate balance gets out of kilter, tension and conflict mount on all sides, within family and community, within the adolescent, and in the zones of interaction between them. Family and community point an accusing finger at the adolescent and say, in effect, "There is something wrong with you; do something about it." The adolescent, in turn, points an accusing finger at family and community. He, too, says, in effect, "There is something wrong with this generation of adults, with our kind of family and community life; do something about it." Thus is sparked a two-way process of recrimination and reproach. Each side blames the other, initiating a circular contagion of accusation and scapegoating. Three themes emerge, which become organized and expressed as a cluster of interrelated, interdependent role patterns, that of the attacker, that of the intended victim of the attack, the scapegoat, and a third role, that of the healer of the conflict.

In the adolescent's struggle to come to terms with his image of self and his environment, he experiences the surrounding disorder of human relations patterns, stretching across a span of three generations, not only as threatening but also as twisted and sick. He strives frantically to serve as healer of his environment. He is driven to do so in order that he may not himself fall ill. In this healing mission, he may succeed or fail. To the extent that he succeeds, he effects a change for the better in family and community. He is thereby satisfied and strengthened. On the other hand, if he fails in the healing mission, the warped, sick forces of his environment persist or are worsened. He is weakened in the effort, rendered more vulnerable; he may then turn delinquent or suffer an emotional breakdown.

I shall try here to explore the theme "Adolescent Struggle as Protest." I propose to tease out of this protest the valid core of criticism, implicit rather than explicit, that the adolescent makes concerning the imbalance, disorder, and sickness in contemporary patterns of family and community life. I shall illustrate this thesis with two clinical case studies. I shall refer to streaks of immaturity that stand out conspicuously in members of the parental generation, to the vicious cycle of contagion that results when the immaturity of adolescents collides with the immaturity of parents, thereby aggravating the disorders of family life. From the inflamed tissue of these relationships emerges a process of pathological healing, a deformation and scarring of the design for family living. Along this path, I hope to search out some useful diagnostic interpretations regarding the contagion of value distortion that pervades the human relations climate both in and between the younger and older generations.

The adolescents of our time are hoisting distress signals. They want the rest of us to know that they are in trouble. The main trends of juvenile disturbance may be specified as follows:

1. A tendency to antisocial behavior, as expressed particularly in acts of unprecedented violence

2. A revolution in sexual mores, shown in a tendency to promiscuity and perversion

3. A wave of contagion that makes an obsession of everything hot: hot jazz, hot dancing, hot rods—a compulsive quest for an ever-new kind of kick

4. A leaning toward overconformity with family and community, or with the peer group; closely associated, a trend toward static-mindedness, a loss of adventure, a loss of creative spark

5. A tendency toward withdrawal, toward a loss of hope and faith, toward disillusionment and despair, with progressive destruction of ideals

6. A failure on the part of the adolescent to harmonize his goals with those of family and society, a trend toward disorientation, confusion, and fragmentation of personal identity; finally, as a result of aggravated disorders of social adaptation, an increasing vulnerability of the adolescent toward emotional breakdown

The core of the problem is epitomized in the adolescent's fierce, often failing struggle to find himself in the near chaos of the contemporary world. He searches for a sense of identity, a sense of wholeness and continuity in a society that is anything but whole and anything but steady in its movement through time. The emotional storms of the adolescent need to be understood not only as an expression of a particular stage of growth but, beyond that, as a symptom of a parallel disorder in the human relations patterns of family, society, and culture. Adolescent behavior needs to be matched, particularly, against the turmoil and instability of marital partnerships, the insecurity of parents, and the disintegrative trends in family life as a whole. The struggle with the wars and wounds of family life leads not to a true recovery but rather to warped healing. Not only are families confused, disoriented, fragmented, and alienated; whole communities often exhibit analogous trends.

The discontinuity, the incongruence, the lack of fit in the relations of individual, family, and community are a critical force in the modern community. "In a few short years," says Hanson, "the solidity of a world of order has vaporized into a nightmare of uncertainty." Sartre speaks of this as "the cinema sheet of naked existence, with no way out, round or through."

Whenever there occurs an eruption of teen-age destructiveness, there is an immediate outcry among the adults of the community; a show of fright, shock, worry, righteous indignation; then talk and more talk. There is a loud, desperate call for action, a program; something must be done. With each such outbreak comes a spate of suggested remedies, such as vocational training, recreational facilities, guidance programs—also physical punishment, stricter policing, and even penalization of parents who are presumed to be negligent. At the peak of such agitation, there is a strong resolve to act, but as is the case with New Year's resolutions, nothing much comes of it. The conviction grows that these measures are mere sops, feeble attempts to plug the hole in the dam. Disillusionment spreads; finally comes the grudging admission that the real problem is not the adolescent alone but rather the sources of disintegrative influence in the sick or broken family. Exactly at this point, the loud talk subsides because no one yet has a proven program for what ails the family. Parents, teachers, and community leaders—all are pervaded by a sense of utter impotence, only thinly disguised. It is this that explains the widespread feeling of helpless resignation and the temptation, shamefacedly, to turn away from the problem. In effect, these waves of panic and agitation are a sort of shadow boxing. People rant and rave, they lash out at the shadow, but are impotent with the real thing, the disorder of family and community life itself.

Yes, there is something deeply wrong, but it is not just with our adolescents; it is with our whole way of life. Our social health shows signs of failing and the effects of this failure cast a long shadow on our mental health.

Now, let me illustrate with two clinical vignettes:

A boy, John, aged fifteen, is involved with several cronies in planning a holdup. This boy is the third of four children, the abscess of the family, the bad seed. The other three children fit well into the family. It is a poor one; its main concern is survival. Otherwise, the family as a whole is dedicated to intellectual and artistic achievement, hard work, renunciation of pleasure for future reward. The family, as family, represents solidarity and sacrifice. John stands out like a sore thumb. He is described as selfish, lazy, impulsive. He is dramatically the black sheep; he threatens the integrity, the values, the continuity of the entire family.

Within the family, John is viewed as the sole criminal. He is treated as if he were on trial. He is indicted as different, alarmingly different. The parents prize scholastic achievement, the importance of reading and knowledge as a way of getting ahead in life. John hates books. He prefers outdoor activities—hunting and fishing. He enjoys using his body, not his brain. "Different people have different ideas," says John. Living inside the family is like trying to stay alive in a strait jacket. He feels humiliated and enraged that his parents indict him as being stupid simply because he does not conform to their goals and values. In self-defense, he asserts that each person is smart in his own way. He declares that his father and brothers are stupid when it comes to life outdoors. He would not insult people simply because they don't know certain book facts. Within the family, he acts dumb. Being viewed as stupid, he isn't expected to see, hear, or listen. Within the family, he feels small, unimportant; he has no voice; he plays dead. He comes alive only outside the family. He says, "I have more fun alone and with other people."

Says John, "No one in this family knows how to have any real pleasure. They are all deadheads." He charges his parents with being hypocritical and self-righteous. There is no real unity between them. Father is against mother, mother against father. Mother has some lively spark, but she chokes it off out of conformity. Father in turn accuses her of associating with shady characters.

The parents are here joined in a tight security pact, but their emotional bond is a loose, unsteady one. The goal of family solidarity comes first. Loyalty to family means sacrifice of personal desires. Beneath their surface expression of unity, however, the parents are divided. Romantically, they are painfully disillusioned with one another. Each competes with the other for the affection and allegiance of the children. The father is bombastic, grandiose, and contentious in his assertion of authority. Behind his facade, he is a weak, frightened, hypochondriacal, martyred person. He is a poor provider. Mother defers superficially to the man of the house, but is secretly contemptuous of his weakness. Consciously, she joins with father in the professed family ideal. At a deeper level, however, she rebels against the rigid requirement of sacrifice as the price of acceptance. She shares with John a suppressed dream of adventure and romance, and subtly fosters his rebellion against father. Father usurps the maternal position with John. Mother displaces her urge to emasculate father onto John. Thus, both parents scapegoat John; they sentence him to exile. John is the sacrificial lamb, on whom is heaped the family's accumulated resentment over the forced surrender of their individual differences.

In another family, a sixteen-year-old girl, Jean, is withdrawn, has no friends, and refuses to attend school. She either barricades herself in her room or emerges to involve herself in belligerent bouts with her mother and grandmother. She threatens suicide and exhibits bizarre mannerisms —a tense cough, twirling her hair, averting her gaze, and wormy gestures of her hands and body. She engages in active hallucinatory communication with the reigning lady in a planet in space called Queendom. Zena, the queen of Queendom, provides her with a Zenascope for this purpose.

This young patient, suffering an early psychosis, moves back and forth between her real way of life on earth with her family and her psychotic way of life in Queendom. The human relations pattern which the patient has designed for her psychotic community reflects, between the lines, her diagnostic indictment of the pathogenic distortions of her real family on earth.

To quote the patient: "Queendom is another star like our sun, and its brightness is of the first magnitude.—I like to visit this planet. It has a mixture, a combination of life.—It has beings that are like living machines and living factories, instead of organisms like we have here on earth. And these machinelike beings don't get their nourishment from the soil. They produce it themselves in factories. I haven't yet found out all the secrets, but these machinelike beings, they don't have emotions. It's a good thing, in a way, because, although they don't have love, they don't have hate and, therefore, they don't have wars or anything like that. It's a sort of like 'all for one and one for all.' (It's more important to get rid of hate, even if you have to do without love.) People don't kill each other in Queendom. They are in a kind of semiorganic state, they're not living and they're not dead. They are sort of half-asleep.—No males are allowed. The beings are not female, but feminine. They reproduce not by sexual means but rather by simple fission. They are self-sufficient, experience no fatigue, have the power of clairvoyance, and yet are strangely sick; they are afflicted with a mysterious disease which gradually rots the body, while the spirit remains immortal."

It is fascinating to speculate on the meaning of the contrast between the way of life in Queendom and the way of life in the patient's earthian family. What may this contrast signify for the illness process itself? What may be usefully inferred from the value clash which is dramatized in the contrast of the two worlds? What is the same and what is different? In Queendom, the patient designs a way of life which merges elements of her earthian family with other elements of change, which she seems to require as a defense against the destructive patterns of her family. In her psychotic world, she remakes life in a special way, altering the whole value system. She erases whatever is dangerous and ugly in her earthian family life and creates a new design for living, an effort at magical repair. The new way of life, though more bearable, does not point the way toward growth and health. These considerations are relevant to the correlation between the emotional distortions of the family group and this girl's psychosis.

In the life of the family group, there is a profound contradiction between the conscious value striving of this parental pair and their actual way of life. The conscious pretext of peace and harmony is thin; it is virtually a fiction. In actuality, the parental couple slides into a pattern that is routinized, mechanized, static, half-dead. In the joined obsessional effort to control the dangers of uncurbed aggression, sex and spontaneity of emotional expression are reduced to a minimum. It is apparent that a basic shared anxiety concerning destruction pervades the whole family, and asphyxiates any natural expression of warm feeling. The values of love and growth are almost totally sacrificed to the interest of sheer survival; all members suffer in their emotional health. In a family of this type, there is a progressive patterning of pathogenic roles: the grandmother in the role of persecutor; the mother in the role of the chronically immature child-wife, anchored in an obsessionally vapid existence and projecting toward her child only a ritual concern; the father, the emasculated, detached intellectual, too impotent and frightened to offer the child any effective protection. The child is given almost no right to eat, breathe, or grow. There is, therefore, a pathological healing of the family's emotional split, progressive reinforcement of a sick pattern of prejudice, scapegoating, victimization of the daughter, and a malignant trend toward regression.

Thus, this young patient is the victim of a cold war; her divided family finds no real solution for its conflict, no effective way of protecting the growth of the family and its members. The patient falls ill in the course of her failing attempt to heal what ails this family.

Whenever in life a human being suffers or is injured, physically or mentally, always there is the question, who is responsible for what? Who is to blame; who should pay the penalty—the individual, family, or community?

When a helpless child is hurt, all society feels distressed. Unconsciously, every segment of the community and each individual member feels accused, and assumes some measure of guilt and blame. Inevitably, the urge is to fend off the indictment, to deny guilt and pin the crime on a scapegoat.

As a rule, society, viewing the child as an incomplete being, excuses him from direct responsibility. However, as he grows older, stronger, and becomes more of a person, family and community tend increasingly to hold him to account.

In this regard, the adolescent poses a special problem. The teenager is a "tween-ager," neither purely child nor purely grown-up, but a part of both; he is in a state of becoming a whole person. Accordingly, he partly assumes responsibility, partly rejects it, and takes it out on his environment. Whatever remains of this responsibility must then be assumed by family and community. When the delicate equilibrium of the changing relations of adolescent and adult becomes critically impaired, the stage is set for a circular contagion of attack, defense, counterattack, scapegoating, and efforts to heal the conflict.

If youth is expected to listen to the elders, the elders must, in turn, listen to the adolescent. We must, all of us, pay heed to the adolescent's implied diagnosis of what is unsatisfying, unjust, and, beyond that, what is twisted and ailing in the patterns of family and community. The growth potentials of the individual, family, and community are profoundly affected by the ongoing struggle to resolve differences and to achieve some kind of tolerable equilibrium. In this struggle, the adolescent may move forward, backward, or sideways. Likewise, family and community may also move forward, backward, or sideways. As the adolescent experiences change and transformation, so, too, do family and community. At any one point in time, the goals and values of the adolescent and those of family and community coincide at some levels and clash at others. In the short view, some areas of critical conflict are inevitable. In the long view, however, what is good and right for the adolescent is likely also to be good and right for family and community. The crucial problem is the conflict of interests, aims, and values over the briefer sector of time. In this phase, how far and in what way does the adolescent accommodate to family and community? How far and in what way do family and community accommodate to the adolescent? Is the clash of aims and values reconciled in a constructive or destructive way? Where there is compromise, is it appropriate? Does it make sense? Does the mutual accommodation foster further growth on both sides, for the emerging adolescent, and for the patterns of family and community? Or, on the other hand, is a wrong compromise struck, and, as a result, a sacrifice imposed, often a costly and painful sacrifice? Which side then pays the piper? Who suffers the sacrifice?

In a stable society characterized by continuity of tradition over generations, the struggle to reconcile transitory conflict is a soft, muted one; in a society undergoing revolutionary transformation, the struggle is noisy and turbulent. In our time, there is a head-on collision between instability and change in the adolescent, and instability and change in the patterns of family and community. There is an unavoidable time lag in the capacity of each to accommodate to the accelerated change in the other. With the galloping pace of change in the goals and values of family and community, the social environment for the adolescent becomes severely fluid, in effect, almost chaotic. As the adults turn confused about who they are and where they are going, the adolescent loses his guide lines. He is continuously perplexed and unsure about where to conform and where to rebel. In our time, the resources of the individual, and the shared resources of family and community, for bringing about a restoration of an effective equilibrium seem to be deficient.

If we now attempt to translate the adolescent's implied diagnosis of the noxious features in the surrounding human relations patterns, we might make the following interpretation. Family and community today fail in some measure to provide a receptive climate for adolescent needs. In human relations, both inside and outside the family, there is little of genuine loving. There is no easy, spontaneous show of warmth and tenderness. There is no cherished touch. People fear and mistrust closeness. They fear and mistrust an open show of emotion, as if all emotion were bad, destructive, even violent. People move apart; they do not feel one another. In the human relations climate, there is a sense of danger, too much danger. The parents and adult authorities in the community are scared. This makes the adolescents doubly scared. The elders deal badly with their fright. They turn their faces away from the threat. They withdraw and seek safety in isolation. They talk out of both sides of their mouths. They do not practice what they preach. They talk ethics, but are themselves corrupt. They say to youth, "Don't do as I do, do as I say." In the face of their single, all-encompassing drive for success, all other human considerations fade away. Competitive strivings run rampant. Each man races with the next, ruthlessly. The world is felt to be a jungle; it is each man for himself. With such opportunism, people become alienated, mechanized, and lose their human quality. The murderous competitiveness of the business ethic invades the private life of the family. The gain of one member is reckoned as the loss of another. Family relations are measured by indices of profit and loss, as in the business world. The goals of power and mastery assume an overweening importance; they submerge the family ideals of love, unity, loyalty, sharing, and cooperation. To admit the need of others or to show tenderness is a confession of weakness. In its place comes the illusory striving for omnipotent mastery and self-sufficiency. Money and position are God. People come to be treated as things. Human relations become, in effect, dehumanized. At another level, there is the tendency to substitute the appearance for the real thing. This is an "as-if" kind of interpersonal reality. It is not who you are, but rather how you look. Everything in human intercourse is reduced to dress and cosmetics. Contact is skin-deep. From still another point of view, the adults lose the art of play. They preserve little of the natural zest and joy of life. They lose the sense of adventure and become workhorses.

To make a fuller and fairer statement of the problem, we would have to turn about and glimpse the other side of the equation. We would have to ask, in turn, what is contained in the struggle of the parents, what is *their* protest, *their* critical judgment of the adolescents, also of the surrounding community? Once again, we are faced with the same question, who is responsible for what? How far do parents blame the adolescents, the community, or themselves? Limitations of space do not permit a detailed look at this other side of the equation, however pertinent this task may be for a comprehensive statement of the problem. We will confine ourselves, therefore, to some limited remarks.

The parents of troubled adolescents are plagued by elements of malignant immaturity in their own characters. Though they may now be in their thirties or forties, they remain in many respects "tween-agers" themselves. The child is father to the man. There is a hangover of pathogenic immaturity in the adults, long after the passing of the teen-age years. We have, then, streaks of teen-age immaturity in the adults, as well as in youth. The end result is a circular contagion of the noxious consequences of elements of pathological immaturity in members of both generations, and contamination of the relations between them. Youth moves into adulthood, marries, and makes children. Making children is an easy and sweet thing, but raising them and meeting their growth needs is quite another. The adults today fear being cheated of the good things of life. They have a horror of aging and death. They hang on by their teeth to the superficial signs of youthfulness. They move heaven and earth to preserve their outer appearance, to keep looking young and attractive. They are obsessed with clothes, dieting, cosmetics. They carry this obsession to an almost grotesque degree, as manifested, for example, in the woman's need to spend hours making up; in the dyeing of her hair, wearing wigs, face lifting, etc. This accent on youthful appearance at all costs proceeds to such an extreme that in the relations of mother and daughter, the daughter cries out in vigorous protest, "I want my mother to look like my mother, not like my sister. . . . I want my mother to be a mother, not a companion or a girl friend or a confidante. . . . I don't like to call my mother by her first name; I want to call her just plain 'Mommy.'" Fathers are no less obsessed than mothers with keeping young; they merely express it in a different way. They, too, expend much energy in looking neat, trim, and youthful. In their middle years, they must impress their employers and business peers with their vigor, their strength, and their indefatigability. To prove their youthfulness, they knock themselves out in competitive sports, in tennis, on the squash court, on the ballfield; aging men chase the pretty young skirts.

In many families, one finds both parents showing the telltale signs of prolonged and skewed adolescent growth. The immature qualities of their struggle extend far into adulthood and even into middle age. One discerns unmistakably the residue of unfinished teen-age conflict—the exorbitant emotional demands, the clinging to unreal, romantic yearnings, the evasion of responsibility, the extremes of dependency and explosive impulsivity, the frantic indulgence in diversion and escape, the divided self, the inordinate leaning on façade, the outer face of personality, the unreadiness for adult commitment to work, love, and loyalty to family.

Unable to move forward to maturity, they act either like frightened children or like all-powerful supermen. They fail to join as effective marital and parental partners. They compete with one another and with their children. Each parent is anxious, conflicted, driven, too busy with his or her own needs to understand and meet the needs of spouse and children. Each wants something different of the family. The family members clash in their image of what the family is and ought to be. The parents set the example and the children follow suit. The family splits into warring camps. Each parent allies with grandparent or child against the other parent. In the emotional interchange among family members, the pain of anxiety and threat stimulates the urge to attack. Offense feels like the best defense. Better to strike fear into the heart of the other person than to admit one's own fear. In a vicious cycle, anxiety evokes aggression, aggression evokes more anxiety. As the family breaks up, one side battles with the other. One member assumes the role of attacker or punisher, another becomes the victim of assault, the scapegoat, and a third member rises to stem the tide of violence; he enters the role of intended healer of the family war. In struggles of this kind, the aggressive member hangs onto his own sanity by menacing the sanity of another. In the long view, everyone suffers. They become, in fact, families without an effective parent. The failure of parents to harmonize and balance functions becomes critical. Ultimately, each member goes his own way; the family falls apart.

With regard to the wider reflections of human relations disorder, there are two points of view. First, that these are inevitable manifestations of a society in transition, the signs of a phase of crisis in historical transformation. From this point of view, it is assumed that in the course of the struggle, the forces of disintegration evoke forces of reintegration. In fact, Talcott Parsons speaks of this as the "disintegration of transition." The implicit assumption is that a new order will ultimately be restored.

The other point of view is different. It is epitomized in the oft-repeated comment, "Ours is a sick society." Society is the patient. The crucial question is not the semantic one: do we prefer to label the human condition as a "society in crisis," or a "sick society"? The really important issue is the quality of healing. In nature, when distortion or sickness occurs, a parallel process of spontaneous healing always emerges. The really vital question is, will the healing succeed or fail? In nature, again, if spontaneous healing fails or a form of pathological healing emerges, there are critical consequences. It is my impression that the danger in the contemporary crisis lies exactly here, in the aggravated risk of either failure of spontaneous healing or in pathological healing. In both cases, the underlying pattern of distortion or "sickness" is critically worsened.

When we consider the implications of the term "sick," we cannot be clear as to what exactly we do mean. Up to the present time, we have tended to one of two extremes. We have examined society in the mass, making a global assessment of the distorted balance of forces in human relations, or, at the other extreme, we have evaluated distortion and sickness as a malignancy inside the single person. Limiting ourselves to the evidence at these two extreme poles, we achieve at best only a vague, foggy conception of the meaning of the phrase, "Ours is a sick society." It seems probable that we can add a useful dimension to the clarification of this problem through close study of the dynamic interchange between the individual and his close personal group environment. It is in this special sense that I discuss the question, what part of the adolescent protest spells valid criticism, a useful diagnostic interpretation of existing elements of disorder and sickness in contemporary patterns of family and community? Only as we become clear as to the diagnosis of this human condition can we turn to the crucial question, what do we want to do about it?

POLITENESS IN A CROWDED WORLD

W. M. Krogman

> Dr. Krogman is a leading authority in the fields of physical anthropology and child growth. He is well known both for his published contributions and for his appearances on educational television in the East. Dr. Krogman is a Fellow of the American Association for the Advancement of Science.

At first glance this is an odd title. Why is "politeness" a problem? Why introduce the word "crowded"? What has "world" to do with it? There is implicit in this title some idea of a form of social behavior oriented to a changing world. We might pose questions such as these:

Is politeness basically interpersonal at the individual interactive level?

Is politeness ultimately at the international level, so that policies as well as behavior are involved?

Is politeness of increasing importance as population Pelion piles on Lebensraum Ossa?

In essence, then, must we examine and evaluate politeness as a concept and as a sociopolitical force in these dynamic and trouble-fraught times?

Before we delve into these, and ancillary questions, let us define "politeness." Essentially we use it in the sense of a pattern of social interaction, beginning at individual level and then extending to group structuring. I think of *thoughtfulness* and *consideration* first here; i.e., we are polite in terms of what our behavior means to the other; we "consider" his good, inherently, in terms of our responsive attitude; we sort of put ourselves "in the other fellow's place" and in so doing invoke, to a degree, the idea of "do unto others. . . ." I think then of *courtesy* which is really a corollary of basic thoughtfulness, yet is perhaps a bit more structured; in our culture we find it necessary to admonish—even to train—the several groups of workers who deal in public services. (There are even rating awards for "acts of courtesy," which should be taken for granted, yet are too often exceptional!) I think of *respect,* even of *deference,* which are attributes of politeness that are usually stratified, i.e., they are differentially related to sex, or to age, or to various status symbols. In this last realm, politeness can slop over into sycophancy and fawning insincerity. Yet I insist that respect and deference are deeply rooted in the impulse to polite behavior, however narrowed or expanded the reciprocal situation may be. Perhaps I might encapsulate here in terms of "the rights of others"—always remembering that "rights" are culturally defined and *do not* mean the same to all peoples. I shall enlarge upon this theme later.

Well, where are we? I think we are ready to accept politeness as a desirable social force at every level of human interactive behavior. It is essentially and intrinsically an *awareness of others* and it involves *adjustive values,* in the sense of a give-and-take situation. I think both the giver (the politor) and the receiver (the politee) are mutual gainers. When I took my first course in sociology some forty years ago my professor startled me by saying, "The more law, the more liberty." This puzzled me until I realized that law is essentially codified human behavior; it, when observed, confers predictability. Hence, in the presence of law, I am reasonably secure in knowing how an observant person will behave and I can react accordingly. So it is with politeness: when mutual politeness is present both parties are in a situation wherein a predictable pattern of reactive adjustment is established. I am not so crass as to say, "It pays to be polite"—but there *are* cultural values in politeness!

How deeply is politeness rooted in man? Is it a gloss, a veneer, an overlay? Must we with the Persian philosopher aver:

> Morals! Conscience! Laws!
> These be dreams of wily fetisheers
> Man, the essential man,
> Still has his fur, his tail, his pointed ears.

Must we, as in Wells's *The Croquet Player,* retreat to a Cains-marsh where an effluvia of fratricide is omnipresent?

I am on the side of the angels of politeness, as it were. I am constrained to think that politeness—in a vaster sense of cooperative, predictive, human behavior—is so deeply entrenched as to take on biosurvival values. It has been said that certain aspects of intelligence are inherited. As an example, if a species of lion became more "intelligent" (in the sense of total efficiency in the hunt), then a species of animal (e.g., the gazelle) sought by the lion would also become more "intelligent" (in the sense of total efficiency in eluding the hunter). This is to say that there are survival values in certain basic patterns of behavior. I think politeness, as defined broadly above, is in this evolutionary tradition, as far as man is concerned.

We have heard much of the *family* as of biologic origin, rooted in mating and begetting, with varying degrees of mate-mate and parent-offspring relationships and responsibilities. *Man is absolutely unique here.* In him is expressed a high degree of *neoteny,* the slowing down of the developmental processes of the birth-to-maturity cycle. Man is the only mammal or primate with such a protracted period of infancy and childhood—a period of relatively complete dependence. Nearly 30 per cent of man's life is in this state. We are learners; we are not creatures of instinct. No other form of life may make this claim! This is why I am prepared to say that total social structuring is an emergent, evolutionary phenomenon. I know that apes have a "society," but, recognizing this, I still insist that social behavior effloresced with the arrival of man and his unique growth potential.

All this demands that we evaluate our ideas of politeness in bio-behavioral terms. With neotenous growth in man, the whole mate-mate and parent-child situation changed drastically. It became more necessary that the mate-mate association be prolonged in order to care for these decelerated offspring. It became more necessary to introduce a dichotomy in shared responsibilities: the male as provider (quite literally bringing home the bacon), the female as keeper of the hearth (certainly, *Kinder, Küche und Kirche,* in that order, were very early the female roles). What I am saying is, of course, that the earliest family structuring in man must have demanded forms of adjustive and adaptive behavior that, in a broad sense, comes under the rubric of politeness.

Let me be specific. I cannot judge, of course, whether a Paleolithic male was polite when he grabbed his female by her crowning glory and dragged her off to his cave—but I'll wager she did not demur too much, and that she implicitly accepted this marital declaration as within the confines of acceptable behavior and, therefore, at least not *too* impolite! But I can judge by other evidence that cultural politeness—as seen in respect and reverence—did appear thousands of years ago. In a cave in Asia Minor, possibly dating to 75,000 years ago, there was found a skeleton of a badly crippled old man. In the rigors of those days he simply could not have existed without care: someone must have killed for him, prepared food for him, done the male's arduous chores for him, and so on. He was, I insist, the recipient of care and affection—of cultural respect akin to politeness. Let us look, further, to intentional burial, with earthly goods and ceremonial objects, as evidence of reverence akin to politeness. Here, inevitably, we blend a social attitude with a religious formulation. Care for the dead is more than politeness in a purely social context; it is basically tied in with the values relating man to his cosmos. So it is that we now have rounded out the evolutionary cycle of man's behavior: patternings intrinsically biological (the family as a mating matrix) have merged into patternings secondarily social (the family as a rearing matrix) and finally into patternings inherently religious (the family as a worshiping matrix). In every possible way we have reason to conclude that concern and care and respect for others have survival value. There are operative forces of selection for social integration and human welfare that it behooves us to observe and to preserve. No one person, no one people, lives in a culturobehavioral vacuum! This was true as we evolved. This is true as we live.

So, logically, we come to *crowding*. It is especially pertinent that I discuss this theme here in California, for, thanks to the late Prof. Alfred Kroeber, we can document the population of this area from prehistoric to modern times. In many excellent studies, employing archaeological evidence, Kroeber calculated the numbers of persons in the aboriginal peoples of California in relation to hunting areas necessary for individual provision and survival. It worked out to a square mile or so per person; beyond this there was "crowding" in the sense of food-to-man ratios. I am quite sure that hunting areas were carefully drawn and as carefully respected—politely, or else! You see, once more all is relative rather than absolute. But what of today—not only in California but in the world? Here we begin to approach absolutism, for numbers and space and food supply are converging upon finiteness. Some chap has calculated, upon present rates of burgeoning numbers, that Homo sapiens must hang out the S.R.O. sign some time in the twenty-second century. Where politeness then?

It has been remarked by many travelers that the Japanese "are such a friendly and polite people." When apprised of this, a Japanese observed that in an area about the size of California, with eighty million people, they just *have* to be polite to get along with one another. Let me give you a personal illustration, at microcosmic level. I have in my growth clinic a small staff of ten, crowded (and what university ever has enough space?) into three rooms. I rarely add to the staff, or make a replacement, until the prospective associate has had lunch with us all and spent a day or so on the premises. The applicant must be acceptable to all in terms of the sum of an agreeable personality. There must be ability, of course; but there must be, too, friendliness, cordiality, thoughtfulness, consideration, adaptiveness all of which can be wrapped up in an over-all politeness. May I point out, at this quite personal level, that the total adjustment often involves a certain amount of ego surrender. When I am polite, when I am the recipient of politeness, I feel that there is an inherent two-way subordination of *self* to *us,* of *I* to *you,* of yielding a certain amount of personal demand or assertion to the group good. I do not say this is conscious, or that it should be—then it may be a smirking affectation. I say it should be relatively unconscious, rooted in the sincerity of the acceptance of group values.

Let me foray into another realm. You know, there are two kinds of cab passengers: the first tell where they want to go, and settle into silence; the second engages the cabbie in pleasant chitchat. (Parenthetically, in the East at least, there's but one kind of cabbie—friendly, garrulous, and often of strong convictions.) I belong to the second class of passenger, for I enjoy talking, *and* listening. You'd be surprised at what you can learn, often in an instructive, even philosophical vein. Several days ago a cabbie and I got onto the subject of "polite drivers." (I am not a car driver, due to visual problems.) He told me the following story: At an intersection he yielded the right of way to another car, even though circumstances did not demand such a thoughtful act. After a puzzled moment the other driver swung into line. At the next stop light the cars were abreast. The driver got out, came over to the cab, and said, "Are you nuts, buddy? Do you belong to some kind of do-good religion?" Still puzzled, and hence irritated, he drove off. It is a sad commentary on our times that common garden-variety courtesy and politeness were not accepted at face value, but had to be regarded with the suspicion granted the unusual. So often, in circumstances like this, we look for a "gimmick" an "angle," or just mutter, "That was a funny deal."

There is, I presume, a logical sequence that is to blame for a picture like this. The sociologists speak of "shift from rural to urban existence," from "primary to secondary contacts," and so on. They are on the right track, of course, in the sense that industrialization, special-ization, concentration of peoples, and total overwhelming numbers have incredibly widened the interpersonal gap between persons and peoples. And this is an anachronism, really, for in time the peoples of the world are but hours apart. But this is only time and space—it is not life and the living thereof. The "good old days," when a person knew many personally and was known by many, are gone. How many people really *know* their neighbors on the upper floors of their own apartment build-ing, except, perhaps, to nod to as they meet in the elevator?

Let us lay aside all the ologies and isms of sociological jargon and come back to the reality of being human. I don't care for time lags, for urbanized anonymity, for the pressure of numbers, for the pace of living, and all such cultural clichés. I *do* care for the fact that, in my opinion, nothing can abrogate, or should deteriorate, the dignity of an individual human being. This is nuclear to being human and all that humanity implies. I go even further and say that it is basic to a uni-versal acceptance that each of us, all of us, owe respect to each and all as in the image of the Creator of all life.

Up to now I have skirted the fringe of the world situation, apart from reference to a bulging population. There is far more to it than "the numbers racket." There are broader and deeper implications of the values held by whole blocs of peoples (we call them nations or national or ethnic groups). I now move into considerations of politeness at the natiopolitical level. In the last analysis we but substitute people-to-people values and behaviors for person-to-person. I admit certain transmutations where numbers are involved, but I do not admit a radical conceptual shift.

In recent years "nationalism" (the autonomy of ethnopolitical groups) has been in the ascendancy. I am not wise enough to answer the "why?" I can but observe that it seems as though the times were right for such cultural upheavals and adjustments. The yeasting of time, people, is evidenced by present-day ferments. Who is to detail discrete ingredients or analyze the cultural chemistry that boils and bubbles in the world today? I leave that to the chancellories of the world. But I can give them one priceless ingredient, one catalyst, that may allay the explosive chemical instability of the international vat—*politeness* in terms of understanding, of appreciation, of tolerance, and of sympathetic and empathetic guidance.

I would ask of politeness at such a world-wide, people-oriented level a number of questions. Is it related to differential status, involving a strong-to-weak relationship? Is it a function of size and of security? May it be interpreted as a sign of weakness or (worse) of vacillation? These are questions almost unique to the United States, for we, of all democracies, are in the role of an active approval or facilitation of national resurgences. In our policies, in our financial aids, in our cultural programs, we are—whether we know or admit it or not—putting politeness to work on a vast scale. We are indoctrinating by precept and by carefully planned and documented advice; we are guiding because we are leaders; we can guide because (even though imperfectly at times) we practice what we preach. We are among the free people of the world; we have a high standard of living; we have technical knowhow. We can—in a literal sense—afford to accord to others a measure of aid and understanding compatible with all the best values of politeness. I must admit, as I survey our policies, that much of it is rooted in the expediency of political alignment (democracy versus communism), and hence the status symbol rears its hydra-head of various entanglements and commitments. I must admit, too, that size, strength, and security are factors to be reckoned with. Our strength is not as the strength of ten because our motives are pure—far from it. But again, I invoke relativity rather than absolutism: maybe our hearts are 75 or 80 per cent "pure," a 20 to 25 per cent level of imperfection in a very imperfect cultural world. This is not to damn with faint praise; it is but to say we've come a long way, but we've still a way to go.

Politeness, like charity, begins at home. Here, too, we've come a long way. Here, too, we've a way to go. I refer, of course, to our own problems of racial and cultural integration, of which that of the Negro looms large and figures in the urgency of the now. Just as King Canute could not command the tide to hold, neither can we deny the surging tides of cultural change. There is a sweep in the tides of man which, taken at the full, leads to great things, in a paraphrase I lay before you.

"Politeness in a Crowded World?" Yes, and thrice yes! But not as a catch-phrase, not as an empty promise, not as the ill-nourishing pap of political expediency, not as the mockery of petty sloganeering—not, please, any of these.

"Politeness in a Crowded World?" How, then? As a conviction that inherent in politeness—*at every level*—is the dignity, the beauty, the grandeur, and, I venture to observe, the divinity, of the human spirit. As a belief that politeness is a way of life and living that encompasses universal laws and values—that all life has equal value in the eyes of God and that in His sight we are all children, one to the other. As an expression of the fact that we, alone of all creatures, have the capacity to compassion, to understanding, to appreciation, and to sharing with all in all.

Am I polite? Are you polite? Are we polite? If we may answer yes, and if we answer affirmatively for all (and please note that I say *if*), then rejoice, for "God's in His Heaven and all's well with the world": at least this is the Grail that may lead us in our quest for good will toward all men and among all men—good will rooted in mutual politeness!

POLITENESS IN A CROWDED WORLD

Moderator: W. M. Krogman

Panel Members: Nathan W. Ackerman, James A. Peterson, Neil J. Smelser

Dr. Peterson My question has to do with epistemology. Ordinarily we would feel that there were two ways in which we would approach any kind of understanding of what was going on in any given segment of society. One would be to understand in depth the norms and the departures from them, studying enough individual cases to understand the dynamics of those cases; beyond that, we would find the incidence of a particular behavior.

But how does Dr. Ackerman know that the United States is all a mental hospital where we are in such a state as to worry so much about what occurs between some adolescents and their parents? On what basis does he generalize on his experience with those adolescents, when every statistical measure that we have refers to another kind of conclusion?

Dr. Ackerman There are times in life when it is precisely polite to disagree most emphatically. The opposite is also true: there are times when certain gestures of politeness constitute the worst possible offense. There are, at the very least, two kinds of politeness, minus and plus. Some years ago, I participated in an Institute on Race Relations at Fisk University, and afterward the dean of Fisk University said on the question of black and white relations, "I don't care what people feel about me being Negro, all I ask is that they be polite." He told me the following anecdote:

He and his wife were ambling down the street on a sunny Sunday morning and approached a crossing. From one side, a beautifully polished, exceedingly expensive black limousine approached, and from the side street a Negro driving the most dilapidated-looking jalopy you can imagine. The jalopy ran into the limousine. My friend from Fisk University was for the moment paralyzed; he had an instantaneous panicky feeling that he was in the Deep South, and that if he went over to protect the poor Negro driver of the jalopy from the anticipated assault by the white man in the limousine, he might himself be very seriously exposed to an assault along with the driver. He decided to wait to see what would happen, even though his urge was to be a lifesaver for this poor Negro and take the dangers on himself, whatever they might be. As he and his wife watched, the Negro got out and began to kick the daylights out of his poor jalopy, launching a tirade, "You terrible thing, how dare you be so impolite with this good white man in his fine, big automobile?" He looked so sincere and so convincing that the rich white man got out and said, "Now don't be so panicky. I am not really angry; I will buy you another jalopy."

I believe that what we are concerned with in the first instance is the plus aspect of politeness, that kind of politeness which opens the way to genuine human consideration and caring for the other. That is a sheer necessity when people are strangers to one another before an empathy unfolds with respect and consideration for the other. Politeness in this very real, positive sense is essential for human survival and we can't do without it. In looking at the program I wonder whether this subject was chosen precisely because there is a question today, "Do we have enough of it?" I think not. I have no figures on this; quite impressionistically it does appear as though the kind of rearing and training of children in our society has moved in a direction of substantial reduction of good manners and of the value of politeness in the positive sense.

On the other hand, there is the minus side of politeness, where it is a sheer ritual, a caricature of genuine respect for the other person. That kind of politeness can bar the way to the opening of genuine empathy, respect, and consideration for the needs of others. We must bear in mind that there are these two kinds of politeness and we want the right one. When it comes to respect for the dignity of another person, again there are two kinds: one kind of respect that is born out of love and another out of fear and hate. In both instances we want the right kind of politeness and the right kind of respect.

Dr. Smelser   I am going to be impolite enough to pose a question that was not answered. Before doing so, however, I will say that during the course of Dr. Ackerman's remarks my admiration for him went up because at the very beginning he said he was not a believer in statistics. During the course of his remarks, it became apparent that he was a firm believer in generalizations.

Those of us trained in behavioral sciences can be firm believers in generalizations and statistics, which creates a good deal of internal anguish.

Dr. Ackerman   When I made my comment about being suspicious of figures I had my tongue in cheek. I respect figures and also feel that the essence for concern in human relations problems is to be careful about the kind of figures we obtain about certain kinds of human phenomena. We check our interpretation of the meaning of those figures with the greatest care. That problem is a little like the question of relations of politness to the meaning we attach to human differences.

From the Floor   Is indeed the arranged marriage a thing of the past? Animal husbandry has thrived on the opposite assumption.

Dr. Smelser   In a strict sense the arranged marriage wherein the spouses were chosen by the parents or members of the extended family, and the marriage was very much tied up with the transfer of property and tying together of two lineages, is a thing of the past. That there are individual cases of marriages that are in fact arranged directly or indirectly is true, but from the standpoint of the predominance of this kind of arrangement it is a thing of the past.

But control over marriage is not a thing of the past, and ways in which structures that surround courtship influence the class of persons who are available for marriage is a very complicated story. The interposition of sorority and fraternity systems has a great deal to do with the control of selection of future spouses. This is not an arranged marriage in the strict traditional sense, but there is an agency tied in with the interest of the parents influencing their choice. It is a different sort of structure in no sense comparable to the traditionally arranged marriage in times past.

From the Floor   Which child is learning to live in the future society: the child whose parents try to make mental anguish tolerable for the sake of the child, or the child whose parents do separate, with ultimate divorce?

Dr. Peterson   Dr. Landis made a remarkable study of this last year and the Glicks studied 500 delinquents. They conclude that children of divorced parents have less trauma than children whose parents stay together but cannot resolve their conflict.

The question is vague because if parents are so concerned for their children, they will take advantage of some kind of therapeutic intervention so that their problems can be resolved. This would be preferable, but comparing a family in conflict with a family that is divorced, the children are affected less negatively by divorce.

From the Floor   Why among all the other things mentioned did Dr. Ackerman leave out any mention of the tendencies of the heads of families in America to turn over to the Federal government so many responsibilities that have always been those of the role of the head of the family?

Dr. Ackerman   I wonder if that question is posed correctly. It is not my impression that parents have turned over in a motivated way their functions and responsibilities over their children.

From the Floor   How do you account for the currently popular concept that the American family is indeed in peril of dissolution, in view of today's speakers' highly optimistic outlook?

Dr. Smelser   The question is to account for the development of certain ideological positions.

Separate from the question of exactly what is happening to the family during this period of continuing and rapid change, which is roughly associated with the changes during and since the Industrial Revolution, the changes themselves create a great deal of discontinuity between generations, between parents and children. After all, one cannot possibly hope to know the same sort of world that his parents or those who lived in other parts of the society knew.

The situation is one of ambiguity. One of the very common responses to rapid change, when society is moving from one form of social organization to another, is to develop a view romanticizing the past. All sorts of images are conjured up: the past family had certain kinds of ideals; the United States used to have a certain type of openness it didn't have before; the family used to consist of calm, sober, hard-working people. This ideology, condemning the contemporary family, looking upon it with such gloominess in contrast with the utopia of the past, is an integral part of rapid social change.

From the Floor Would Dr. Ackerman please comment on Dr. Peterson's view of the function of the significant difference of divorce in society? Is this not at least partly a way of giving up, drifting, and denying the problems of marriage, rather than trying to solve them?

Dr. Ackerman I am not nearly as sanguine concerning the outlook of the contemporary family as are the other two speakers in this panel. They both sound like the voice of reason; they sounded so fair and objective that I decided I did not belong to their fraternity. They are rational; I, being a psychiatrist, am irrational, and responding to the moods of the times. In that sense I think the fundamental issue is not whether to adopt an attitude of good cheer and optimism for the future of the family or to sink into the deepest kind of pessimism, cynicism, and despair. I think that is a loaded question.

The issue is rather one of the degree to which we together can conscientiously work toward a gradually increasing clarity and accuracy, not only in our view of what is wrong with the modern family but also of what is right. This is self-evident as soon as we shift our focus from the one-to-one relationship of patient and doctor and the study and treatment of a disturbed person to an examination of the family phenomenon as it pertains to mental health. We must be as fully concerned with the preserved forces of emotional health in the family as we are with those other forces that can make the members susceptible in one or another degree to a breakup.

From my point of view this cannot be an either-or approach in any sense. We have to weigh the good things against the bad, but that does not justify us, as professionals, in holding a bright, defensive position, advising the rest of the community that things are just swell, nothing much is happening, and we can be fully confident that the family is going to survive.

I share the conviction that the family is the absolutely indispensable unit of living. This is the same as saying that the human is a social animal. We can't do without a family; it has been tried in Communist China, Soviet Russia, and elsewhere. Efforts to treat the family as an iniquitous entity no longer with any functional use and superfluous in modern society are all wrong, in my opinion.

Therefore I am convinced the family is here to stay, but that is not the issue. The issue is to face up to what things are wrong in the contemporary family, stack them up against those things that are better, and then see what we can do about it.

Dr. Smelser I echo Dr. Ackerman's sentiments that it is the moral responsibility of persons who investigate and think about these major social problems to weigh the good with the bad and to be courageous in offering both diagnoses and recommendations concerning contemporary social problems such as those associated with the family. But I must also underline the responsibility of those who are in the position of investigation to be as careful and judicious as possible in gathering the relevant facts.

I think our responsibility extends even further in this area because of the tremendous range of statements, ranging from Pollyanna to Cassandra. The obligation on the serious investigator is all the greater in this sense.

Dr. Krogman I would like to ask Dr. Smelser this: what about the full-time working mother of a very young child who delegates her influence and authority to the sitter or child-care person?

Dr. Smelser We must consider the data. There is a really low percentage of participation in the labor force by women with children under five. There is a very high participation rate before children arrive and after the onset of schooling for children, but between these periods there is a dip, and the participants in the labor force at this level are clustered in the lower-income levels and also among broken families.

Considering the psychological effects on the child of the absent mother in infancy, I would be more concerned about the psychological effects on the child of an absent mother if this situation were more widespread. I think the presence of a close, durable, and predictable relationship in the very earliest years is as important a thing as a child can have. On the other hand, I wouldn't say that in every case the absence of a mother from an infant's life is going to be catastrophic. In order to determine this we have to ask precisely what are the alternative forms of care offered in any given case.

Dr. Krogman As a carry-over from the previous session, would

Dr. Ackerman comment on the possible development of psychological and emotional ability and maturity that is offered the child in adolescence by a controlled environmental identification such as is offered by the Chinese commune system, contrasted to the conflicting ideals and image figures in our society?

Dr. Ackerman   It appears to me that in a society which changes at a very much slower pace than our own, there is much less tension, conflict, and change in values regarding the control pattern or the authority representation of the family than is the case in a time of social upheaval and extremely rapid changes, both in patterns of the wider community and in patterns of the family.

Perhaps there is a simple, self-evident principle in child rearing. If a child to begin with has a basic sense of belonging to the family and feels secure and valued as the creation of a love bond between the parents, there is no problem of disciplining that child. Even rather rigid controls are assimilable by the growing child without too much conflict.

The trouble begins where the child is lacking in basic value for the self within the matrix of the family. In such circumstances the child is never sure of his standing in the group and his value for the parents and himself. In that situation discipline can become a perfectly awful problem.

From the Floor   I have been concerned with the opinion that the male role in our society is being subverted by the dominance of the female in the home, the male being relegated to the wage earner and the female being the dominant figure in social, economic, and emotional factors.

I would like to ask: Is this producing any noticeable effect on the children of today who grow up seeking security in future positions that offer them so-called fringe benefits? In others words, has it taken the spirit of initiative, creativeness, and adventure out of our children who are going to grow up today?

Dr. Peterson   The question of the shifting roles of men and women and the impact on a child is really the heart of this issue. The male instrumental task and decision-making role has necessarily been divided and shared with the female because of the mobility of the male's occupational role. She pays the bills, gets the screen door fixed, and makes decisions about the children when he is not there. The structure of the modern family means that this role has changed.

When father comes home angry and won't speak to the children, the mother assumes the role of what Dr. Parsons terms an expressive leader, saying, "Well, you know father is tired. He had a hard day. He loves you." In the nuclear family, we have found that the man likewise must invade the woman's role and become expressive if he is going to meet her needs.

We just finished a study in which we contrasted the total adjustment of the marriage with the degree to which these roles were shared. We found that those families had an optimal kind of adjustment where the man had a great deal of expressiveness, emotional warmth, concern, and tenderness, and where the woman was competent in some of the male roles. None of us is competent to say how far this invasion or transverse role has gone, but it has not gone to the extent that the nuclear family demands this dual playing of roles so that the child will feel the goodness of the warmth of devotion between husband and wife. My reaction would be entirely negative to the question: What kind of family would give the child the kind of security of which Dr. Ackerman has spoken?

Some of the hostility between men and women stems from the development of change between them. Men tend to lag culturally and to accept the equality intellectually, culturally, and sexually that the woman comes to play. There are courtship customs during the developmental stages of young people which are such that they often provoke different types of hostility between the two. While the basic contribution may be one of congruity and better relations between husband and wife as we leave traditional roles, the transitional costs are such that a great deal of hostility develops, and we see a great deal of this in family alignments.

Dr. Ackerman I couldn't possibly contain myself when the idea of a passive male in the contemporary community came up in the staff meeting of our Family Mental Health Clinic. It is always the females on the staff who refer to the passive male; I never hear the male members of the group express this, and it gets me mad.

The biggest delusion that has ever been foisted upon the profession or community is that there is such a thing fundamentally as a passive male.

Critical changes have taken place in the family. The position of the male in the family has shifted very markedly for many reasons, and it is this that has led to the caricature of the father figure as something between a vagrant, an absentee landlord, and a sap.

A psychiatrist said to me the other day, "I am very worried: there are so many husbands who don't control their wives the way they should, and the wives go plumb crazy."

Two related factors are both delusions in my view: one is the passive male and the other is the dominant female. If it is true that the men in our community are becoming less masculine, it must be equally true that the women are less feminine. If this is so, we must be going backward and people are behaving either as children or as supermen; if so, they ought to look into the reasons why.

The fact is that men are too accommodating when they agree that women are the stronger half of humanity, and they ought to ponder why that is so.

In my view, the woman who appears superficially to be over-aggressive, dominant, and castrating is trying to fill a void made by the retiring attitude of the man in the family. What she really wants is for the man to be stronger and more protective, and she is just needling him to be the man he should be in the family.

From the Floor This figure of 16.6 per cent divorces represents an actual number of marriages that end in divorce. Isn't this very much like an iceberg with a small amount above the water? What is the amount under water that for apathy or one reason or another does not come to divorce, and yet represents really an unhappy married situation? I wonder if this is what Dr. Ackerman had in the back of his mind when he was talking about the generally unhappy American family.

Dr. Peterson We are not wholly happy with divorce statistics, but they are the best indicators we have. There are a number of individuals who for religious, psychological, and other reasons are unhappy but elect to stay in the family. I assume this was always true; we have no way to find out what was the level of contented, happy, and well-adjusted families ten, twenty, or fifty years ago compared with today.

As Dr. Smelser said, there is a difficulty in accepting change and adjusting to a time of social invention. However, in the presence of such difficulty, the important thing is, what kind of attitude do we have toward divorce as the effective way of helping individuals move out from that situation so destructive to their own personality and to the personalities of their children? We may feel morally that there is some great evil about it and might keep people in an unhappy marriage and damage the children; we could move out and be more permissive, accepting divorce as functional in the situation.

In our society, with its changing marriage forms, we of necessity have to let boys and girls make their own marriage choice. This is part of their growth, participating as individuals in individual decisions when they get out in society. When they make their own decisions, without the help of parents, however, those decisions are often the result of great sexual and erotic attraction, of romantic idealization, and sometimes of pregnancy. Very young marriages do not take into account very real factors of value differences. To hold individuals like this in a marriage because of the value of marriage itself is to perpetuate conflict, struggle, and damage to children. It is far better to let these individuals try again because what we have discovered is that their second effort is usually wholesome and they stay together. But if we legally and moralistically oppose this kind of adjustment technique on the part of society, then actually we are doing damage to the institution of the family in society. In this view, divorce becomes actually a technique of improving family life.

From the Floor We are always concentrating on repairing the damage that we do to ourselves in poor marriages. Couldn't there be more emphasis on family life education in high school, to act as a preventive medicine to young people, so they will start good families with a good foundation for our government and our country?

Dr. Peterson We are without really adequate measures of the difference between individuals in their marriages who have had a full course of family life education and those who have not. What indicators we have suggest precisely that, because of the complex and confused nature of marriage choice, where young people had a better opportunity to make a choice their marital relationships were better.

In California, the state is considering the possibility of a statewide campaign in family life education. In Indiana, some 65 per cent of the high schools offer it, and Dr. Kirkendall will discuss later his experience in Oregon, where they have a very comprehensive program of this kind.

In a period of rapid social change, it seems to me that if young people are at least aware of these role shifts and the kinds of challenge in modern marriage, they will take these into consideration before marriage, rather than later. When this happens, there is bound to be some impact on the marriage rates and the divorce rates.

PART THREE

THE DECISIVE YEARS

Chairman: J. Fenton McKenna

Prominent in the field of drama production, Dr. McKenna has held important positions in organizations connected with the creative arts. He is Chairman of the American National Theatre and Academy and is active in a number of organizations dedicated to the understanding of the creative arts in relation to human endeavor.

The third session considered three critical facets of the family. The opening speaker concerned himself with the impact of sex education as a factor strongly influencing the young married couple in relation not only to themselves but to their children. The adaptation of the father was the next subject; the adaptation from the natural state and the stresses of modern urban living were evaluated as important causes of both family stability and friction. The third speaker took a positive view of the values and potential of the many roles played by the wife and mother; in her view the complexity and conflict has been overestimated. These three topics were discussed in the panel to follow, in which the competition between generations, which has given rise to so much concern, was set in a new light of family evolution and as such was found to be overestimated except where traditionalism overruled acceptance of today's social matrix.

SEX, EDUCATION, AND FAMILY STABILITY

Lester A. Kirkendall

A member of the Board of Directors of the National Council of Family Relations and the author of many works on family life, Dr. Kirkendall is one of the leading authorities on sex education. One of his recent works is entitled Premarital Intercourse and Interpersonal Relationships.

May I, as I start, remind you of that delightful little verse by Ogden Nash,

> In the beginning
> Life was not complex
> Then the amoeba tore itself apart
> And started sex.

The inclusion of sex as a topic for consideration in this symposium, "The Family's Search for Survival," is encouraging. Sex may eventually be regarded as a respectable subject for serious discussion. The fact that the title first suggested for my talk was "Sex and Family Conflict" is less encouraging. As usual, sex was approached in a problem context, and as a threat. Recently I participated in a mental-health workshop which focused on three topics: suicide, sex, and drug addiction. Now I am again scheduled to participate in a symposium sponsored by an association of professional workers. The title of the symposium?—"Sex and Suicide"!

So the title originally proposed, "Sex and Family Conflict," was quite in context. It reflects the prevailing view that sex is menacing, a potential destroyer, a disruptive force. That it could represent a fulfill-ing, integrating, potential-releasing force is seldom envisioned and hardly at all understood. It is most often understood and accepted as having that potentiality within a happy marriage, and as it involves husband and wife.

For a married man or woman who may feel an attraction for a person of the opposite sex not his spouse, for individuals who are alone and/or are likely to remain unmarried, for urban families with small children who may be molested, or with teen-agers who cannot be closely supervised, sex often represents an oppressing threat. For such persons and families sex is an evil spirit always ready to violate the sanctity of the individual, disrupt marriage, disgrace the family, and impose bur-dens of secrecy and guilt. In general, sex, other than within marriage, is something to be suppressed and subdued, not something to be en-couraged and enjoyed. Ordinarily it is associated with irresponsibility and exploitation, rather than responsibility, creativity, and fulfillment.

Must sex always be regarded so fearfully? Can it enhance and en-rich life when properly related to the age and the life pattern of the individual?

I believe it can, but, if so, some very different concepts are needed.

If sex is to be a stabilizing rather than a disruptive, disturbing force in family life, our thinking and attitudes must undergo an evolu-tion similar to that which has occurred in the field of health.

Professional health workers have quite clearly moved from a con-cern with curing diseases to an emphasis on preventing diseases and maintaining health. Now the most enlightened medical and health practitioners are taking the next logical step. They are asking how a human being can fully develop and satisfyingly realize his potentialities. That is, "How can he live, not only having good health but so as to utilize and enjoy that health to the maximum?"

The Preamble of the World Health Organization embodies this broader point of view when it says, "Health is defined as a state of complete physical, mental and social well being, not merely as the absence of disease and infirmity."

We need, so far as sex is concerned, to explore and traverse the same path. We have been concerned—yes, preoccupied—with curative measures. Agencies like the Salvation Army and Florence Crittenden

Homes have worked at extending aid to and rehabilitating unmarried mothers. Orphanages and foster homes have been relied upon to care for illegitimate children. The white slave traffic has been outlawed. Prophylactic stations have been set up by the military services, and campaigns waged against prostitution. Through the curative approach, evils have been curbed and their consequences ameliorated.

But we are now moving somewhat beyond this. As Dr. William Genné of the National Council of Churches of Christ in the United States noted in a recent conference, the need for a positive educational program has been recognized. Literature has been written and courses developed which have blazed the trail toward a more responsible management of sex, both before and during marriage.

Dr. Genné added, "We must grant that some of these early attempts were crude and cruel in that they used fear as their principal motivation." However, they did go beyond mere curative efforts—they were working on the preventive side, and gradually they have been taking on a more positive coloration.

But now, just as the medical and health authorities have faced the challenge of developing positive, creative, fulfilling health practices, so are we faced with the same challenge in the area of sex. How will and can we deal with sex so that, rather than being a disruptive, disturbing factor, it can fulfill and release potentialities? How can it be made to contribute to satisfying, enriched living at all periods and stages of life? This is the issue with which we must concern ourselves, and the issue which I will discuss.

I am not now advocating or presupposing any particular pattern of sexual behavior. At this moment the advocacy of specific sexual practices or patterns is beside the point. I am concerned with establishing different concepts of sex than commonly exist. Once this has been done the place and significance of sex and its implications for family stability can be explored, but first certain reevaluations and reassessments of sex must take place.

First, we must rid ourselves of the common, paralyzing fear of sex which leaves us both tongue-tied and blind to reality. We have been thoroughly imbued with the idea that the sex urge is very demanding and overpowering in its strength. It stands ever ready, we feel, to break through any and all barriers to its expression. Our only safeguard is a continual vigilance, a constant repression, and a never-ceasing guard against arousal. Should arousal occur, the individual in his attempt to find physical pleasure and release may override all social regulations, and damage or destroy both himself and others in his attempts to obtain sexual satisfaction. On the one hand we have a neurotic fascination and obsession with sex, and on the other a fearful, recoiling attitude toward it. This crippling, contradictory interpretation of sex, unfortunately, has been widely accepted. Many professional people and certainly the lay public generally hold this point of view.

The evidence does not support this concept of sex; in fact it suggests a contrary point of view. Sex is at times a powerful urge, but so are other of our impulses powerful. Sex is as subject to direction and management as our other appetites and desires. It is much more amenable to direction and control than we have recognized.

Second, the conditions which historically have dictated and supported our conventional sexual morality have changed greatly over recent years. Traditionally those patterns of sexual conduct accepted as moral and virtuous have been buttressed by citing certain dire consequences of nonmarital sex as possible outcomes, i.e., unwanted pregnancy, venereal diseases, and public and family ostracism and disapproval. These threats have been almost wiped out by medical and technological advances in the fields of (1) contraception, which markedly cuts down on the likelihood of pregnancy; (2) prophylaxis, which makes disease less dreaded; and (3) mobile, urban living, which makes isolation and anonymity possible. Concomitantly we have experienced a marked relaxation in the rigor with which public opinion disapproves participation in nonmarital sexual activities.

Other modifying forces could be mentioned, too, for example, the declining power of religious authority, cultural intermingling which brings many kinds of differing practices and value systems into direct contact and conflict, the shifting role of men and women in their relations to one another.

Other forces could be mentioned, but let us say simply that sexual morality, so much a central concern of the family, can no longer be dealt with realistically in the conventional framework. A way of looking at sex and morality which takes into account current forces and circumstances must be found or the present chaos and confusion will simply be compounded.

Third, sex must be put in a broader context. "Sex" usually connotes genital union, or some practice which leads to orgasm. In order to move toward a broader concept let us forget sex for a moment, and begin by thinking of the importance of love and affection as so commonly expressed through physical closeness, and through touch and embrace.

Recently two pediatricians wrote:

There is abundant confirmation for the thesis that the infant and young child require consistent love and care from a mother (or mothering person) in order to develop along eminently healthy pathways. As a corollary of this thesis, it can be stated that prolonged separation from such a mother-figure is an extremely trying and potentially life threatening experience for the child involved [1].

The family especially affords the opportunity for this need to be satisfied in infancy, the time in life when this satisfaction is especially important. The desire for physical contact, for closeness and nearness, is present at all periods in the life cycle, however. This is a way of communicating acceptance, of providing assurance, of giving the basic sustenance from which mature, fulfilled personalities are nourished and developed.

Dr. Aaron Rutledge, psychotherapist at the Merrill-Palmer School, writes:

Just as food and oxygen are necessary to grow and maintain a body, nearness is essential to a healthy personality. . . . One of the best ways of counteracting some of the basic insecurity in youth today would be providing, in the first days and weeks of life, a great deal more of the skin-to-skin nearness of calm and secure mothering in loving, tender, physical ways [2].

In his presentation Dr. Ackerman made essentially the same point.

As I have already said, the need to experience nearness extends beyond infancy and childhood. It is something we all need, something which has meaning and is precious to us throughout life. Regardless of age, when we like someone, we feel an impulse to touch, to come close to that person. Parents lift their children, embrace and caress them. The children like this, and so do the parents. People of all ages engage in hugging and caressing, and find it meaningful.

We encourage small children to comfort each other by touching and embracing. "Billy is unhappy, Linda. Put your arm around him." We are pleased with these expressions of closeness and nearness as long as they are confined to husband and wife, or involve prepubertal children. However, once puberty is reached and the expressions involve males and females from different families, sexual connotations enter. Now the touch-embrace expressions, or even the desire to experience them, become threatening because of the fear of sexual involvement. Their expression may create feelings of uneasiness or even panic in the parents. Irresponsible sexual expression, casual intercourse, and the first steps toward promiscuity are visualized as likely outcomes.

The individual who feels this desire for physical nearness is often equally uneasy. In our culture, if male youth are involved with each other in physical touching or embracing, the panic is even more severe. Homosexual tendencies are suspected, or even assumed to be present. Boys themselves avoid such demonstrations like a plague, and if they should engage in them are likely to feel their masculinity impugned, and to feel guilty and disturbed over what has occurred.

Let us put it this way. We live in a social climate which has made us fearful and suspicious of our tender impulses. These feelings have been tied to our fears and rejections of sex and so have been renounced, but in this very renunciation we have become even more the captive and pawn of that which we have feared—ungoverned sexuality.

Three things may now be said. First, following this logic, sex may be recognized as a natural culmination of a touch-embrace continuum based on affection and a desire to reach out to others. It is not, of course, always experienced in this context. Second, the desire to touch, for closeness, which will ultimately manifest itself in sexual union, represents an essential aspect of the mature, loving individual. The absence of such desires would reflect deprivation indeed. Third, the reasonable satisfaction of such desires through infancy and early childhood is essential if the individual is to develop the capacity to guide and direct his various impulses and appetites. Specifically, the individual who has been loved and appreciated as a child and who has had his desires for physical nearness satisfied is ordinarily able to guide and direct his sexual impulses in adolescence and adulthood. He is not driven by obsessive sexual needs. Such a person is much less likely to exploit others, to be heedlessly self-centered than the person who has missed such experiences. When he does seek sex he is more likely to look for it in a relationship setting, rather than accepting it as a casual, isolated sensory outlet.

Maslow made similar observations about the relationship between sex and love in self-actualizing (highly mature) people. He said, "Sexual pleasures are found in their most intense and ecstatic perfection in self-actualizing people. . . . [Sex] is often a profound and almost mystical experience, and yet the absence of sexuality is more easily tolerated by these people. . . ."

He commented upon the "self-actualizing person's simultaneously enjoying sex so much more intensely than the average person, yet at the same time considering it so much less important in the total frame of reference. . . ."

He also said:

An excellent parallel may be made between this and the attitude of these people toward food. Food is simultaneously enjoyed and yet regarded as relatively unimportant in the total scheme of life by self-actualizing people. When they do enjoy it, they can enjoy it whole-heartedly and without the slightest tainting with bad attitudes toward animality and the like. And yet ordinarily feeding oneself takes a relatively unimportant place in the total picture. These people do not *need* sensuality; they simply enjoy it when it occurs [3].

I believe Maslow is correct in his views. This point is so important that I wish to tie it into my argument more closely. I wish to show the important implications it has both for family living practices—for sex education—and for family stability. I wish to suggest the place which I believe sex-sensory satisfactions have in the total picture.

I will begin with a question. Should parents be concerned about children and adolescents who seek sexual-sensory pleasures from their own bodies? The most obvious expression of this, of course, is through fondling of the genitals and genital play in children, and full-fledged masturbation in adolescence.

Parents traditionally have taken a very dim view of this. Professional educators have warned them against genital play and sexual experimentation in children. They are told to avoid leaving children too much alone and unoccupied, and to divert the children's attention if they are found touching their genitals. The obvious purpose has been to keep the children from experiencing sensory pleasure through the handling of their sex organs.

For years adolescent masturbation has been sternly disapproved. This attitude has been changing in recent years until now it is common to find assurances from authorities that masturbation is not harmful unless worried about, or "is excessive." Even so, one often gets the impression from these statements that the speaker would prefer this experience did not occur.

Now, however, the view has been advanced that autoerotic or sex-sensory pleasures have a positive value and should receive approval. For example, Dr. Walter Stokes, in the 1961 meetings of the National Council of Family Relations at Salt Lake City, August, 1961, stated, "I believe that the time has come to throw out all traces of our ancient negative ideas about masturbation. Instead we should defend it and recognize the importance it has in any rational concept of personality structure and social relations."

Remarks made at this time indicated this view did not find ready acceptance among professional family life people.

Parents are also quite hesitant, even resistant, to such an endorsement of masturbation. This results, I think from a lack of perspective of the problem. It seems an advocacy of masturbation, of threatening sex-sensory experiences, for no significant reason.

I find myself agreeing with Dr. Stokes, for I feel that if individuals are to develop their fullest potentialities and live as mature, stable individuals, certain needs must be satisfied. This means that different kinds of satisfactions are necessary, and in certain amounts. Each individual will exert strenuous efforts to attain the various satisfactions he needs, and if he cannot fulfill them in direct, positive ways, he will move in directions which are ordinarily regarded as deviated and distorted.

Here I could turn to a number of students of human behavior for lists of human needs. I choose, however, to paraphrase Erich Fromm [4] in setting up my own list.

One needed satisfaction is derived from a reasonable sense of mastery and from the experience of having the power to control and direct at least some situations. There is a real and important satisfaction in meeting and overcoming trials and tribulations. Another satisfaction comes through experiencing achievements and accomplishments which are meaningful to the individual, and still another through adventuring forth in a manner which gives the individual the feeling that he is growing, opening new doors, and is "going places." Another real and important satisfaction derives from the sacrifices he makes for others, from the unselfish giving he does.

Another needed and legitimate source of satisfactions comes from the body and its sensory processes. Satisfactions come from physical exertion, from "big muscle" activities, the pelting of water on the body in a shower, or massaging or stroking parts of the body. Who doesn't enjoy the feel of clean sheets on a bed, or the cozy warmth of an enveloping blanket? These are all sensory pleasures, frankly and openly enjoyed.

The erotic sensations which come from genital fondling, the sensory pleasures of masturbation are other sources of satisfactions derived from the body and its sensory processes. Through these experiences the individual learns what to expect from his sexuality. His curiosity is satisfied and he stands to gain a feeling of poise and a sense of assurance concerning his sexual endowments. And of course, we have already spoken of the extreme importance to the individual of the pleasure of physical nearness found in a warm, affectional relationship with those important persons about him (for children, their parents; for adults, their children, spouses, close friends). What is more meaningful than the satisfaction the individual finds in close body contact with a person he loves? Sexual pleasure, achieved through various activities or methods, is a way of receiving satisfaction through the body and its sensory process.

The danger to individual and family stability comes when satisfactions can be obtained from only a limited number of these sources, and little or none can be obtained from the others. When the individual is too sharply restricted in the sources from which he can gain his satisfactions, he is likely to engage in bizarre, distorted, deviated behavior in an effort to obtain the needed satisfactions, or depend on certain satisfactions unduly and excessively.

Thus the person denied affection, or who feels a failure in his efforts to achieve and master, may seek satisfaction through sexual promiscuity. The individual who has been denied sex-sensory satisfactions may become obsessively interested in sex, or concentrate disproportionately on some other sensory satisfaction while denying an interest in sex.

My contention is that a person who finds himself well-supplied with satisfactions obtained through love and affection, through meaningful and creative achievement, through experiences in mastery, through giving and sacrificing, through the feeling that he is "growing" and expanding his horizons, and through some sensory satisfactions is in an excellent psychological position. The satisfaction he will need to obtain through thrill seeking will not be much, and the demands he makes on sex-sensual pleasures will be reasonable enough that he will neither be gluttonous nor exploitive, nor will he endanger the rights of others.

An adolescent who has received adequate satisfactions from such nonsexual sources as I have mentioned can usually be content during his adolescence or even young adulthood with some experience in masturbation, some fantasy, and the normal sensory satisfactions which come through the erogenous zones of the body. The important thing is that the child or the adolescent not be made to feel guilty and evil over the satisfaction he does obtain in this manner, and that his various nonsexual sources of satisfaction be regarded as meaningful and kept accessible to him. He is likely to know that he could enjoy something more, but he will not be driven to it. He may, of course, go further, e.g., non-marital intercourse, because he finds this easily possible and because in terms of the mores he knows, going further is acceptable.

This approach makes it possible for marital sex to become one of the ways in which spouses may communicate with and enjoy each other and their life together. Sex need not be utilized for retaliation, to hurt, to control, or as a bribe to compensate for some other deficiency, as is sometimes the case both with marital and extramarital relations. It can become an aspect of life which has been integrated into the context of living, and can thus stabilize the family rather than threaten it with disintegration.

To put the same idea in another way, and more simply and pointedly, what we need in our families are more expressions of love and compassion, and fewer of rejection, hostility, and aggression. Aldous Huxley, in this same symposium in 1961, raised this issue very pointedly when he asked, "How can we increase the amount of love in the world? How can we elicit from individuals their potentialities for friendliness and for love, and how can we, if possible, do something constructive about their potentialities for violence and aggression?"

He noted that whereas "all the great religions have insisted upon the importance of love—Christian charity or Buddhist universal compassion—very little has been done in the way of suggesting means whereby love can be actualized on a wider scale and in a deeper way."

Huxley then turned to one of the primitive cultures described by Margaret Mead and commented on their practice in which

[The] mother as she nurses her child strokes the child so the child is enjoying both the pleasure of eating and the pleasure of being stroked and being in contact with the mother, and while this is happening the mother will rub the child against other members of the family or against anybody who happens to be around, or even against the domestic animals which roam about the huts, and murmur, "good, good." . . . it is . . . a curiously ironic thing that it has remained for this primitive people . . . to have invented an effective way of creating a prejudice in favor of friendliness [5].

I have now spoken of sex and family stability. Where does sex education fit? In order to accomplish the kind of integration about which I have just been speaking, our sex education program must be characterized by certain features.

1. *Sex education must be, first and essentially, human relations education.* Historically we have relied on a dual approach. On the one hand we have attempted to study human beings and human behavior devoid of any linkage with the sexual impulse. On the other we have attempted to treat sex as something apart from the rest of our humanness. Tearing it from context, making it something to fear and disdain, we have disregarded sex when we could, and given it the shortest possible shrift when avoidance techniques have broken down. What is

needed is an educational approach which regards sex as an integral aspect of the human being. A concern for satisfying human relationships should form the core, for we are first of all human beings, then male or female.

But we definitely are male and female; let us not forget that. Also let our educational programs reflect this by incorporating the necessary knowledge and insights about sex. In this way we can be helped to understand and accept sex as an inseparable part of our humanness.

Envisioning a program of such breadth means, of course, that discussion of it could be endless. I shall, therefore, make two observations which I see as central to the views I am advocating.

First, one can hardly deal with sex and its relationship to family stability without considering concepts of morality. The family is inevitably deeply concerned with the moral standards of its members. One of the reasons parents fumble so badly in helping children with sex is their fear of stirring sexual desires which will result in sexual involvements. Educational programs designed to help stabilize the family must, therefore, deal realistically with the foundation of sexual morality since, as I have indicated, the conventional approach has, in my view, lost its meaning.

And what is this foundation? I believe that moral judgments must rest upon a concern for the quality of interpersonal relationships which are created by our attitudes, feelings, and behavior. As I have written:

Whenever a decision or a choice is to be made concerning behavior, the moral decision will be the one which works toward the creation of trust, confidence, and integrity in relationships. It should increase the capacity of individuals to cooperate, and enhance the sense of self-respect in the individual. Acts which create distrust, suspicion, and misunderstanding, which build barriers and destroy integrity, are immoral. They decrease the individual's sense of self-respect, and rather than producing a capacity to work together they separate people and break down the capacity for communication [6].

This is not a narrow concern for a two-person association or a tightly knit little in-group. A good relationship leads its members toward an increasing acceptance of others, and others to an increasing acceptance of them.

Neither does it submerge the individual to the group. It recognizes rather that a reciprocating process is involved. Man is a social animal, and he finds his greatest satisfactions and his greatest miseries in his relationships with his associates and the group. But the group has an equal stake in the individual, for no person can relate himself to others with maturity and loyalty except as his own basic personal needs are satisfied. This principle of reciprocity must be remembered and carefully developed, for only by doing this can the proper balance be attained.

My second observation is this: A sound educational program should stress the importance of the family as an open rather than a closed or provincial unit.

I refer first to openness in expression of affection and sentiment. This point I have already discussed.

The second openness is receptivity to the consideration of all kinds of ideas and experiences. This is an essential feature in the development of interpersonal relationships, for relationships are created, not handed us full flower. They are hammered out in the give-and-take of daily living, and annealed in the tolerance and understanding which can come from full and free communication.

The concern of parents for protecting children and youth from strange and alien thoughts or against issues which have emotional impact is so strong that the family becomes a citadel of conservatism [7]. It becomes, also, a unit in which personal feelings, experiences, hopes, and frustrations are submerged and hidden by the various family members from the awareness of the others. This is especially the case when right or wrong issues are thought of in terms of a rigid pattern of specific acts. Such an approach divorces behavior from a concern for motivation and responsibility, and excludes open consideration of alternatives. The approach to moral judgment which I have suggested requires a freedom of interchange which few families attain.

This kind of openness and the freedom of dialogue it demands may offer hope for producing people who have the outreach and flexibility needed to meet the demands of change which are now flooding upon us. It is no longer possible to retreat to the privacy of the isolated family unit as a way of ensuring a particular pattern of moral conduct.

Let us now turn specifically to sex education and comment on some features which should characterize it.

2. *Sex education should extend through the life cycle.* Two common concepts of sex education are very stultifying. First, it is thought of as for children and youth, and second, as being mainly biological information. For children, sex education is generally synonomous with reproduction education.

Actually, since we are sexual beings throughout life, there is learning to be done so long as we are alive. The prevalence of marital sex difficulties has pointed to the need for education during the early adulthood years and through middle age. The educational need at this level has been met primarily, however, by suggesting counseling when difficulties have arisen—again effort directed at the curative level.

So far as old age is concerned, sexuality at this stage of the life cycle has for all practical purposes been ignored.

One circumstance of importance has masked the need for adult sex education. Adults no longer participate in any realistic or effective way in the sex-socialization processes of youth. Few parents go much beyond providing biological-reproduction facts. More extensive cross-generational discussions concerning sexual matters are badly needed. If adults dealt realistically with the sex-socialization processes of youth, the importance of sex education throughout the life cycle would be markedly increased. However, the consideration of sex in relationships, its use as play, as a method of communication, or as a unifying experience, if it comes to youth at all, must come through literature or by the way of peers. Sex in this context is not discussed directly with youth by adults.

Ordinarily we consider the participation of parents in the socialization processes of their children as increasing the stability of the family and/or of the society. It is probably too much, however, to expect other than a few extraordinary parents to deal with the sex-socialization process as it relates to their children. Most parents are too deeply enmeshed in fears and inhibitions which render them both blind and mute when it comes to dealing with their children on sexual relationship matters.

It is, however, important that adults do participate in the sex-socialization of youth and that they do it verbally and in face-to-face situations. This points to the need for much more and better sex education at the adult level, at least for these special educators, than most persons have. Furthermore, other adults, especially parents, must have an equivalent education or they will never permit what needs to be done with youth to be done. This also points to a third characteristic of sex education.

3. *It should help in modifying and dispelling taboos which interfere with communication and socialization.* Specific taboos need to be dispelled. One, for example, prohibits adults from acknowledging their own sexuality, unless it is done with frivolity or in a spirit of braggadocio. For an adult to acknowledge his own sexual perplexities or speak of his own sexual experiences in a serious discussion is almost unheard of. Were I to do that from this platform, at the best it would be considered bad taste and at the worst a defiant or an exhibitionistic gesture. Yet I am a sexual being with sexual experiences from which I have learned both about sex and about life. Why not accept this fact—a fact which is true of all who are listening?

If adults are to give effective help in the sex-socialization of youth, this kind of openness will have to come.

Another taboo which must go is the one which interferes with the provision of straightforward yet realistic analyses of sex. We are flooded with all kinds of lascivious, inciting stimuli from the mass media and through commercial channels, but refuse to let comprehensive, objective discussion develop in our families or our schools.

Adults generally find it impossible to approach the sex education of youth in a manner which might imply that the choice of whether they remain sexually chaste is theirs to make. This keeps the adults from considering both the pros and cons, the advantages and disadvantages of particular courses of action.

Yet my experience in working with youth indicates that an objective approach which recognizes that youth has a choice to make moves us toward several important outcomes. First, it makes the adults realistic partners with youth as they work at the resolution of their sexual dilemma. Second, it enables each adult to take a position of his own without seeming to be dogmatic or biased. Third, it allows sex to be looked at in a positive as well as a negative framework. This kind of balance is badly needed.

I have been impressed with the extent to which our teaching about the nature of sex and its use in relationships has the same overtones as our teaching about disease. We are preoccupied with the dangers of both, with ways of immunizing against them and with other avoidance techniques, and with detailed discussions of the threats they pose. Teaching in this negative context, we speak of both sex and disease with conviction and in detail; teaching in the positive context we have generally spoken of the positive meanings of sexual expression, as we have of good health, in very general, nonexplicit terms.

We do, of course, find very positive but highly generalized statements about the place of sex in relationships, marriage, and the family. For example, we find Bertocci and Millard [8], in *Personality and the Good*, saying, "What requires special note at the human level is that there is room for much experimentation and learning and therefore for much artistry in the expression of the sexual urge."

But we hesitate greatly in spelling this out in any way for youth and in the family. In fact, what probably happens is that children and youth are dealt with in such a way that by the time they reach marriage they will have much difficulty in attaining and practicing the "artistry" of which Bertocci and Millard speak.

Details could be added and various points extended. But perhaps I can summarize with this sentence. Once we can dispel our fear of sex and build into our personal and social attitudes genuine feelings of warmth and acceptance toward others, our sexual problems will be on the way to solution, and the potential contribution of sex as a stabilizing influence in family life will much more likely be realized.

References

1. Thos. E. Reichelderfer and Lawrence Rockland, "Maternal Deprivation and the Effect of Loving Care," *Clinical Pediatrics*, 2:449–452, August, 1963. The concept of maternal deprivation has been reappraised in *Deprivation and Maternal Care: A Reassessment of Its Effects*, Geneva, World Health Organization, 1962, Public Health Papers No. 14.
2. Aaron Rutledge, "Missing Ingredient in Marriage—Nearness," *Social Science*, 36:53–58, January, 1961.
3. A. H. Maslow, *Motivation and Personality*, New York, Harper & Row, Publishers, Incorporated, 1954.
4. Erich Fromm, "Values, Psychology and Human Existence," in Abraham

Maslow (ed.), *New Knowledge in Human Values,* New York, Harper & Row, Publishers, Incorporated, 1959.

5. Aldous Huxley, "Human Potentialities," in Seymour M. Farber and Roger H. L. Wilson (eds.), *Control of the Mind,* New York, McGraw-Hill Book Company, 1961, pp. 60–76.

6. Lester A. Kirkendall, *Premarital Intercourse and Interpersonal Relationships,* New York: The Julian Press, Inc., 1961.

7. Philippe Aries in his book *Centuries of Childhood* (New York, Alfred A. Knopf, Inc., 1962) traces in an interesting way the development of the family during the sixteenth and seventeenth centuries as an isolated, private unit, and its withdrawal from the pattern of communal living. One of the forces giving impetus to this movement was the desire to escape the licentiousness of the times and protect the morals of the children.

8. Peter Bertocci and Richard M. Millard, *Personality and the Good,* New York, David McKay Company, Inc., 1963.

THE AGONY OF CONFORMING:
THE MALE PARENT

Russel V. Lee

The founder of the Palo Alto Medical Clinic and the Palo Alto Medical Research Foundation, Dr. Lee is well known as an innovator in the organization of medical practice. He is active in the support of programs for elderly people. He also serves as Medical Consultant to the Agency for International Development.

To speak of the necessary adjustments a male parent must make if he participates in the institution of matrimony as the "agony of conforming" is really putting it a little too strongly. All human relationships require sacrifice. We must determine, for ourselves and for society, whether they are worth the price. And having made this determination, conformity with the conditions imposed is in order. Properly this adjustment should be made without agonizing about it. Such an adjustment, however desirable, is unfortunately not possible for many people, and unquestionably many males caught in·the trap of matrimony suffer grievously. The high divorce rate in California (1 in 2) would indicate that a certain measure of relief is available to many people.

In spite of the unilateral awards in favor of the female in most divorce actions, men really suffer more in marriage than do women. The state is less natural for the male; his responsibilities are greater; he contributes more and gets less out of marriage than the female. This side of the question is seldom stressed. The indignities and sufferings of the female are amply publicized. The question as to whether these sacrifices are desirable for the person and for society will not be considered here since they have been amply covered by other speakers. The origin and the nature of the male difficulties in adjustment to marriage will be the topic of this paper.

First of all, considering man as he is, as a mammal, monogamous marriage is a bizarre and unnatural state. In a state of nature the normal buck, bull, stallion, or primate collects, dominates, protects, and impregnates as many females as he possibly can. This has had beneficial genetic results in assuring that the species will be bred from the strongest and most aggressive males. Only the strong procreate. The human male certainly shares the same aspirations and drives as do other mammals. To circumvent this tremendously powerful natural instinct is indeed a traumatizing experience, and does entail a certain agony of conformity. Not that such conformity is by any means the universal pattern of human male behavior. Polygamy has been widespread in the history of the human race and the concept of strictly observed monogamous matrimony is a relatively recent one. And even where this institution of monogamous matrimony is the recognized pattern of behavior, most studies (Kinsey et al.) indicate that strict conformity is not entirely universal. But this sort of nonconformity is no help in mitigating the agony, for it is additionally traumatizing to go contrary to accepted social practice. There are those today who seriously advocate some return to a system of polygamy and give a number of reasons for it, in addition to the point we have made of the biological tendency in this direction. As everyone knows, there is a surplus of marriageable women. And in addition to the actual numerical preponderance, the situation is made worse by the number of males who for one reason or another are disqualified for matrimony. These disqualifications include impotence, homosexuality, alcoholism, psychosis, and economic disability. These defects, while of course common to both sexes, are much more serious when they occur in the male. Impotence and homosexuality proverbially disqualify a male for marriage, but not a woman. A psychotic male in marriage, or an alcoholic one, is sure to make a failure of it, but many a borderline psychotic or alcoholic woman is sufficiently protected in the haven of matrimony to make a go of it. The first source of agony therefore can be said to be the violence that marriage does to the biologically ingrained instinct for promiscuity.

There are other sources of agony, partly instinctual and partly psychological, that particularly affect the male rather than the female. One of these is the strong drive for freedom from restraint. The primitive man roamed far and wide and freely as a hunter; the woman cowered in the protection of the cave. The home is usually the world to the woman; often it is a cage to the freedom-loving male. The English club and the old-time (no women allowed) saloon represent attempts in the modern world to achieve this freedom. The nagging female's "Where have you been all this time?" is part of the agony of lost freedom.

The loss of the hero role in modern marriage does violence to another deep-seated male psychological drive, i.e., the desire to be a hero. Again, when the primitive male dragged the game home to the family, he was a hero; when he killed his rival and stole the rival's women, he was a hero; when he, one male, dominated a harem of many females, he was a hero. Now, with equality established, the male as a hero, except perhaps in the prize ring, is no more. And he misses it. A few smart wives still use the "Aren't you wonderful?" technique, but this is a pale substitute for the pedestal of the hero. These are examples of psychological agony inherent in the marital state.

But in spite of this so-called equality of the sexes and in spite of the tremendous increase in jobs for women outside the home, the male in marriage is still subject to certain economic pressures which can be agonizing indeed. He is supposed to provide for his family. Some males cannot. All fathers feel the implacable pressure upon them at all times to "bring home the bacon." There is no more agonizing experience, I am sure, than for a husband and father to be in the position of being expected to provide and finding that in spite of his efforts his family is in want. For the 10 per cent or so who can never be successful, matrimony becomes a nightmare compounded if it also includes paternity.

Paternity has always been highly regarded, perhaps only slightly less highly than the reputedly pleasurable act of procreation which must precede it. Since the dawn of history elaborate precautions have always been taken by the male to assure the legitimacy of his offspring. The possession of many children, particularly if they were males, was a source of strength if you were a fighter, a hunter, or a farmer; and in the olden days these were about all you could be. And when, as in Carl Sandburg's village of liver and onions, "everything was just the same as it always was," the sons, instructed by the father, followed in his footsteps. No more. Except in the case of lawyers and doctors, rarely do the children follow their father's profession, and when they do, modern advances have been so spectacular that they far outstrip their parents. There is no joy in having a son who does everything better than you do and lets you know it. So, the old, old satisfactions of parenthood are converted into more agony for the male parent.

And to all this another agony has been added—not strictly pertinent to the matrimonial state but very much a part of the system. This is the agony of survival to the period of "ugly age and feeble impotence and the cruel disintegration of slow years." There was a time when the old man was honored. He was the titular head of the tribe, and his counsel was sought. Even when senility supervened, his wanderings were treated with respect and scrutinized for possible hidden meaning. No more. He now is a problem—for housing, for medicare, and for whatever will get him away from the children. The end is the lonely agony of the useless old man for whom the modern matrimonial problem makes no place. A victim of success.

The aptitude most responsible for the survival of the human race has been and is his adaptability. Men live in icy igloos under the midnight sun and survive; they live naked under the blazing tropical skies and survive. The race has survived the most atrocious and bloody tyrannies and veritable nightmares of misgovernment. Men have adapted themselves to all these extremes and to various unnatural conditions. They can adapt, and have done so, even to matrimony with all its inherent restrictions. And we do move forward. The amazing advances in medical sciences, transportation, communication, and methods of killing ourselves have not, to be sure, been matched by advances in government or in sociology. But such advances are possible. The better understanding of man's psychological make-up and of anthropological and evolutionary influences upon his behavior makes possible new approaches to these common problems of living. The potential of modern science is fabulous. We should not stress the difficulties without considering the possibilities. There is no more reason to regard the institution of matrimony as static than other human institutions. We do well indeed to consider what is wrong, but we do better when we consider what we can do to make it right. Let us not agonize about it for a moment. Let us rather, applying what we know, build an institution that preserves and develops the great values in marriage, and go on to something better fitted to human capabilities and human weaknesses.

HOUSEWIFE AND WOMAN? THE BEST OF BOTH WORLDS?

Hilda Sidney Krech

Well known for her novels To Wake in the Morning *and* The Other Side of the Day, *Mrs. Krech has also contributed many articles to national magazines. She is coauthor of* The Many Lives of Modern Woman *and* The Best of Both Worlds: Housewife and Woman.

Scoldings, dissections, and revolutionary proposals—all about modern woman—have been filling the air for ten or fifteen years. They've also been filling newspaper columns, books, TV programs, learned journals, not-so-learned journals, and symposia from the Vassar campus to the University of California Medical School. Surprisingly, words about modern woman have been flowing and symposia have been gathering at an increasing rather than a decreasing rate. More surprising still, a lot of people seem to be willing (sometimes even eager) to hear about her once again. I find myself challenged to say something new about her before the subject (and the discussers of the subject) are exhausted.

When I considered the concern—the serious, frivolous, scientific, sympathetic, and sometimes furious concern—that's been lavished on modern woman, and most especially modern American woman, I started wondering why she remains bewildered and bewildering, why her dilemma remains unsolved. And I was struck by the fact that we haven't all been talking about the same American woman.

Most of the talk and most of the criticism has been lavished on the more or less privileged, more or less educated, presumably intelligent woman. She is the one who has encouraged the word "discontented" to be linked with the words "American woman." She has been forced to add the feeling of guilt to her feelings of frustration because so many people for so many years have been telling her how lucky she is. And she is. And she knows it. But still—but still what? Her dissatisfaction is about equally divided between what she *does* do and what she *does not* do.

Speaking with women who are quite happily married, one often gets the feeling that housework and child care are both too much and too little for each one of them; too much because they take all her time, energy, and thought during the period when her children need constantly to be fed, clothed in clean clothes, fetched and carried, and tended to in one way or another; too little in that she'd somehow been led to believe that she would be using her time and her talents and her energy quite differently—at least for a portion of each day. All through school and, for many, through college as well, these talents—whether artistic, intellectual, practical, or human—have been respected and encouraged.

Though, deep inside, there is nothing she would rather do than be a mother, she often feels, while her children are young, like a drudge. When they are grown, she is a has-been—sometimes feeling that she's a *has*-been without ever really having *been*. She is no longer needed as a full-time mother, yet no longer able to be whatever it was she set out to be all those long years ago. For, contrary to polite and gallant statements which suggest that simply "being a woman" is a vocation, this is not the case.

To make such a woman's discontent stronger still, the truly lucky woman is married to a man who does interesting, challenging, perhaps useful, and sometimes lucrative work which often gets more challenging and useful as the years go by, while her work gets less challenging, less useful. Growing up, she didn't wish she were a boy. She doesn't wish now that she were a man. Yet something is wrong with this picture of the luckiest woman in the world.

In answer to the countless articles, speeches, and books which have painted just such a picture, *The Saturday Evening Post* recently ran an article defending the American woman, refuting the countless statements which accuse her of being "lonely, bored, lazy, sexually inept, frigid, superficial, harried, militant, overworked." The adjectives are those of the authors, Dr. George Gallup and Evan Hill, who made a survey and then described what they call the "typical" American woman.

(Though one-third of the married women in America are employed outside the home, and though nearly 15 per cent of women over forty-five are widowed or divorced, the authors specifically state that these women are not "typical," and, therefore, they are neither discussed nor included in the composite picture. Getting ahead of my story for a moment, I'd like to point out, also, that Gallup and Hill's typical American woman is forever young, forever surrounded by young children.)

The charges against the American woman are untrue, say Dr. Gallup and Mr. Hill. She is happy; she is content; she wants only "the simple pleasures"; her family is "her whole life." Their typical wife sums up her situation by saying: "If I don't want to do the dishes or laundry right now, I can do them later. My only deadline is when my husband comes home. I'm much more free than when I was single and working. A married woman has it made."

Her house may be cluttered, but her mind is not. Only half of the women interviewed read books at all; only 13 per cent consider "intelligence as a prerequisite in husbands." The only reference to the life of the mind in this article quotes the typical wife as saying: "I spend my spare time broadening my interests so I won't bore Jim." So I won't bore Jim! Apparently she doesn't mind boring herself. She may be free, she may be content, but if she is indeed typical, I can't help considering the possibility that modern woman, for all her modern appliances, isn't modern any more.

The Saturday Evening Post's typical woman, at any rate, knows neither the nagging worry of poverty nor the nagging pull to be part of the activity and thought of a world that extends beyond her eventually made bed, her eventually cleaned house. But, of course, *she* is not the woman that commentators have in mind when they talk about "frustration" or when they describe the Radcliffe diploma mildewing over the kitchen sink.

And when we read the *Report of the President's Commission on the Status of Women,* the emphasis is on a still different woman, a woman who works because she has to or because she wants to give her children a better life. She cannot be called a career woman, for she is likely to do clerical work or saleswork, service work, factory work or agricultural work, and only a small percentage of the women working in our country today are in professional or managerial jobs.

Clearly, it is impossible to speak in the same breath about all these kinds of women, at least in any meaningful way. Even within these groups, of course, there are enormous differences between individual women—differences in ability, in intellect, in preferences, in temperament, in values. But about these differences remarkably little is ever said. This tendency to speak of women as though they were interchangeable units like the parts of a Ford is one reason why (for all the talk) woman's dilemma remains unsolved.

A second reason is that while we've been talking, the picture has been changing. For women have not turned a deaf ear to this talk. If anything fascinates them, it's the topic of themselves—a fact which suggests a close relation to the rest of the human race—and they have tried to follow the suggestions, heed the warnings. While reflecting the feminine condition, therefore, some of the commentators have, at the same time, helped to shape that condition.

"Womanpower"—the word and the commodity—was discovered during World War II. When the war was over and womanpower was no longer needed in factories and hospitals and schools (or so they thought), many voices started urging women to go home, stay home, and like it. In 1947 Marnya Farnham and Ferdinand Lundberg wrote *Modern Woman: The Lost Sex,* in which they predicted: "Close down the commercial bakeries and canning factories today and women will start being happier tomorrow."

They were talking to the young women of my generation who had started out to do great things—not only the privileged and the educated; all kinds of girls were going to have "careers" in those days. Then, as each girl married (always to her great surprise, for she never dreamed she was going to meet George or Bill or Frederick, or if she did, she kept her dreams to herself), she would "throw over her career," as she liked to put it. Sometimes she did so cheerfully, for she knew there really was no career in the making, sometimes reluctantly because it was nearly impossible to keep on after her first or second child arrived. She became a housewife or, as she tended to put it, "just a housewife."

Dorothy Thompson created a new cliché or, at the very least, gave new life to an old one, when she pointed out in 1949 that a wife and mother should never feel apologetic for being "just a housewife" because that homely word means that she is a professional "business manager, cook, nurse, chauffeur, dressmaker, interior decorator, accountant, caterer, teacher, private secretary" all rolled into one. "I simply refuse to share your self-pity," Miss Thompson told the American housewife in the *Ladies' Home Journal*. "You are one of the most successful women I know."

The following year, in *The Atlantic Monthly*, another woman journalist wrote an even angrier article. Agnes E. Meyer not only tried to reassure those women who spent their entire time being mothers; she fiercely denounced those who made some effort to be something in addition to being mothers. She wrote:

Women must boldly announce "that no job is more exacting, more necessary, or more rewarding than that of housewife and mother. . . . There have never been so many women who are unnecessarily torn between marriage and a career. There have never been so many mothers who neglect their children because they find some trivial job more interesting. . . . The poor child whose mother has to work has some inner security because he knows in his little heart that his mother is sacrificing herself for his wellbeing. But the neglected child from a well-to-do home, who realizes instinctively that his mother prefers her job to him, often hates her with a passionate intensity" [1].

Each time such a statement was made, and they were made often, it was a shot in the arm for those who had felt aimless and demoralized, who had, to quote one of them, "begun to feel stupid with nothing to contribute to an evening's discussion after a solitary morning of housecleaning and an afternoon of keeping peace between the children." Now they were able to face themselves with more self-respect, for they were doing the most important job of all. What's more, they were able to look with *less* respect at their friends who had outside work or interests.

As for these women, the ones involved outside the home as well as within, many of them were intimidated by the strong voices. It was confusing to them, even frightening, to be told they weren't good mothers, to be accused of preferring their outside activities to their children. Increasingly, therefore, many turned their full attention, their full energies upon their little families and shut the door on the world.

And so, while the canneries and bakeries did not literally close down, the spirit of this advice was taken; and many highly educated or trained women have been making their own bread, putting up endless little jellies. But according to the latest attack on the subject, *The Feminine Mystique* by Betty Friedan, these women aren't happy at all but are slowly going mad and battering their children's heads!

Nobody's happy about them either. The consensus at the Vassar symposium held in the spring of 1962 was that: "If the performance of college women from 1920 through World War II has been somewhat disappointing, the mental attitudes of young women since World War II are alarming."

This kind of criticism came from looking inside woman's head and heart. Looking at her from the outside came another kind of criticism— first, the accusation that having no other interest in her life, she latched fiercely onto her children, ruining them, being a "Mom." More recently, still another kind of criticism has been coming: that she hasn't been pulling her weight. "A Huge Waste: Educated Womanpower" is the title of a typical *New York Times* article, this one published in May, 1961. Two years later, under the heading "Tapping a U.S. National Resource," came another *Times* article concerning itself with "the educated woman."

This past summer Max Lerner wrote an article called "Let's Draft Our Girls," and he meant all kinds of girls. Four years earlier *Harper's* had published an article in which Marion Sanders discussed the possibility of drafting not only girls before they become mothers, but also strong, able women after they have finished their full-time mothering, unless they are already engaged in work that has some value. Though her style is gay, almost frivolous, and I don't think Mrs. Sanders seriously wants a draft for women, she does want us to pull our socks up and is quite serious both about the need for teachers, nurses, and social welfare workers and about her scorn for what she calls Non-

Work or Sub-Work or Redundant Housewifery—the pointless tasks with which so many middle-aged women fill their lives.

As an example of women she would *not* exempt, she tells about a hospital ladies' auxiliary in Long Island which "boasted that its 900 Pink Pinafore Volunteers last year spent 51,280 hours reading to sick children, giving patients alcohol rubs, and running a gift shop. This averages out to a little more than an hour a week per volunteer—scarcely time to don and doff the pinafores."

In addition, then, to the great differences between different women (about which too little is said), and in addition to the changes constantly taking place in our attitudes and in our ways of living, there is a third reason we've been progressing so slowly in gaining insight into modern woman—her role, her function, her old dilemma. Many true things have been said, but since they aren't all said at the same time, we get part of the picture in one strong statement, another part in another (seemingly contradictory) statement. We never get a full, accurate picture in one glance, but a blurred and confused impression. And while I can't say everything all at once either (not even the things I do know, let alone the things I don't), I'd like to give an example of what I mean.

One often hears that too much is expected of the American woman. "How can she be wife, lover, confidante, companion, hostess, cook, seamstress, floor scrubber, purchasing agent, teacher, chauffeur, child analyst?" ask her defenders.

But in Mrs. Sanders's "Proposition for Women" she speaks of middle-aged and older women with "time for leisurely jaunts to the lonely housewife's dream world of 'shopping'—so different from 'marketing.'" And she describes clubs with many meetings which "did not contribute to anyone's enlightenment since their programs revealed no coherent purpose. (January: Flower Arrangement. February: The Bright Side of Menopause. March: Whither the UN?)" Women caught up in such activities spend an enormous amount of time telephoning to arrange similar meetings which, in Mrs. Sanders's terms, is "Circular (or self-perpetuating) Puttering, a form of Sub-Work."

Both kinds of descriptions are valid, although it's obvious that both apply more accurately to middle-class and upper-class women. What people *don't* always recognize, however, is that the demanding descrip-

tion applies only to a woman's early years when her children are young
and she is in constant demand, that the idleness comes later and, worse,
it comes gradually, imperceptibly. Most of us have heard a great deal
about this bonus of twenty, thirty, or even forty years women now have
because they stop bearing children at an earlier age and they live—with
health and vigor—much longer than people have ever lived before. And
though we're still floundering, are not yet sure exactly what we want
to do with this bonus and how to plan for it, many girls and young
women are completely unaware of it. This may be hard to believe; but
the one sour note in the otherwise sweet *Saturday Evening Post* article
is that Dr. Gallup and Mr. Hill report the women they interviewed
could not imagine having their children grown and out of the house,
leaving them jobless. They had simply never given a thought to this
eventuality.

And so women were scolded for going out of the home and then,
more recently, they've been scolded for staying in. The next logical
step is to urge women out of the house and into high-powered careers
on a par with men's, thus bringing us full circle, back to the feminist
days. I'm afraid this step is coming. Whether advertisements follow
public opinion or make it I don't quite know, but I've noticed a small
straw blowing in the wind which may be significant, the beginning of
a trend. After years of picturing lovely ladies who beam with joy while
cleaning their toilet bowls or waltzing around the living room with a
roll of Alcoa Wrap, some advertisers are taking a new tack. One blouse
manufacturer has announced a new advertising campaign addressed to
the 24,584,000 "Wonderful Women Who Work." Going even further,
a different shirt company recently ran an ad picturing a girl as a naval
architect and running a caption which said: "Man's world? Bah!
Women are in everything."

The girl is extremely pretty and looks about eighteen and is totally
unconvincing as an architect, naval or otherwise. But when I think of
the other kind of ad, I realize it's not the unconvincingness that's new,
and I wonder if, after pushing housewifery to the limits, they're now
going to push for "a career for every girl." Look out for that swinging
pendulum; here we go again.

What really alarms me is the strident voice, the strong note of
resentment in Betty Friedan's *The Feminine Mystique* when she asks

why women are always supposed to be satisfied with second-string careers and second-level positions. Having said that, I suppose I've put myself on the spot and had better explain why *I'm* satisfied. Am I being wishy-washy? Or have I boldly taken the position of defending "the radical middle"? I'll say what I believe and you can decide.

I believe that only the rare, truly exceptional woman with way-above-average ability, energy, and drive can—while maintaining a home and being a real mother to several children—achieve a full-fledged career. It takes enormous flexibility and ingenuity, for the children *do* come first, and women *do* move when the husbands are transferred on their jobs, and they don't have their mothers living nearby or maiden aunts or maids to lend a hand when the unpredictable but inevitable complications arise. In our society, husbands carry the main financial burden of supporting the family, whether or not their wives have salaries. And in the same spirit, whether it's a matter of tradition or instinct, wives are usually the ones who carry the main responsibility for keeping things running smoothly at home, for being emotionally supportive to their husbands as well as to their children.

We have to face the fact that for all these same reasons, it is extremely difficult to work out even a half-time job or profession or avocation. Why, then, should anyone bother? And why should I believe this to be a sound and satisfying course for a great many women in our time? If someone has strong, specific interests, proven ability, or a shining talent, it may be worthwhile; but why should other young women go out of their way to seek goals, to seek spheres of interest and activity? Aren't they just looking for trouble? In a sense, yes; it may seem that they're deliberately choosing the hard way and that I'm egging them on.

By not making a deliberate choice, however, by drifting along as so many have been doing, being buffeted by the changing winds of social pressure, present-day women who are in a position to choose haven't found their lives hard, exactly, but too many have found them empty, purposeless. Deliberately making their lives hard by adding all sorts of do-it-yourself chores—from paper hanging and upholstery to weaving and preserving—has been tried by many but has turned out to be the answer for relatively few. Not only is it artificial, but it puts something of a strain on the marriage relationship to ask a woman to

live in a homespun, horse-and-buggy age while her husband continues
to forge ahead in a Dacron, Acrilan, jet age.

However, since so many traditional functions have gradually been
taken away from mothers—not only the weaving, canning, and baking
which many of us would cheerfully forego, but even teaching children
about sex and sewing and social problems (whatever happened to
mother's knee, by the way, and all the things a child used to learn
there?)—it's obvious that unless she and her life are to become empty,
something must be substituted.

As long ago as 1950, Lynn White, Jr., former president of Mills
College, recognized this problem clearly. In his book *Educating Our
Daughters*, he said:

> If the housewife no longer pumps water from the well, she must be
> sure that the city water supply is pure. She no longer wrings the necks of
> barnyard hens for dinner, but an honest meat inspection in the interests of
> public health affects the health of her family. Her children learn their
> letters at school rather than at her knee, but in return she must work for
> the P.T.A.

Mr. White saw the question and he gave us one answer. But I believe that in considering it the *only* answer, we may have lost as much
as we gained. By calling "homemaking plus volunteer community work"
the ideal pattern for modern woman we are threatened with a new
kind of standardization. During the years that girls have been educated
much as their brothers and their future husbands, they have come to be
appreciated as individuals. Parents and teachers, too, have recognized
and have even emphasized individual differences, drumming home the
idea that there are all kinds of ways of being a valuable person, that
"different" doesn't necessarily mean "better or worse." When a girl
marries, is she supposed to forget all this and learn, just as girls learned
in the past: *this* is the kind of life a good wife and mother leads; this
and no other?

There is a second fallacy in the "homemaking-plus volunteer-
community-work" formula—at least when it is recommended as a suitable formula for most women. In the old days each mother had (using
Lynn White's own example) to haul each pail of water into the house
and had to wring the neck of each chicken. But the way things are

now, we don't need *all* mothers working for pure food and drug laws, for fluoridation or antifluoridation, or even for the PTA. Women going into these volunteer efforts soon find out that not all of them are needed. It soon becomes clear that the purpose of much of their work is occupational therapy—not for others but for themselves. Wanting to be useful, many flit from one volunteer or creative activity to another—one year marching for diseases, the next year making mosaics out of broken bottles, the next year being crazy about mental health.

Since the family itself has shrunk, it's true that certain community concerns have taken the place of certain family concerns. We might say that today's extended family has, reasonably and legitimately, been extended to include the community. But different women can make different contributions to the community—both because different women are different *and* because all sorts of things are needed and duplication of effort is tremendously wasteful. Nor are all contributions measurable by the same standards. Some, such as pure research or pure art, cannot be evaluated at all by most of us. And I wish we could just accept that, as we do with much of man's work, not making a woman feel guilty about or accountable for any work she does which is not clearly contributing to her family—or her extended family, the community.

Now that I'm nearing the end of my paper, I'll make three more wishes. I would like to see less distinction made between the woman who must work for financial reasons and the one who has decided to work. The borderline is so hazy, so vague that only in cases of extreme poverty or where no husband is present and employed can one say that this woman simply must work in order for her family to survive. Beyond that who can say whether women are working for necessities or luxuries? Is a washing machine a necessity or a luxury? Is a college education for her children a necessity or a luxury? I maintain that this is for each couple to decide.

Making a sharp distinction between women who must work and those who have decided to work leaves out of account the powerful but often ignored phenomenon of "mixed motivation." Certainly, in most cases, the second income is needed or at least warmly welcomed; but there are other satisfactions, too, whether it's a feeling of usefulness, of accomplishment, or simply the human contact to be found in any store or office.

In the eyes of many people, saying that a woman *must* work for financial gain casts a reflection on her husband. The question is raised: "Can't he support her?" Ironically, reflections are also cast on the woman who has chosen to work. The question is raised: "Does she really love her children? Is she a good mother?" For all these reasons, then, I think the question of whether a woman is working through choice or necessity is often meaningless and destructive.

My second wish for women is that a less sharp distinction be made between the paid and the volunteer worker. I would like to see a climate of opinion in which the paid woman worker is neither apologetic about needing the money nor arrogant about being "a professional." Were it taken for granted that everyone works to capacity, the professional would become less defensive and the volunteer would become more professional—that is, she would feel a strong and continuing sense of responsibility toward her work and her colleagues, a sense of commitment which would keep her from quitting whenever the going got rough (or boring).

My third wish, then, is just that: a climate of opinion in which it's taken for granted that women will do something with their training, their abilities, their energy once their children are half-grown and they have free time at their disposal. First of all, there is the obvious waste of "womanpower" which was first noticed during the war, but was then forgotten until relatively recently—perhaps because of Sputnik and our "educational lag," as the shortage of first-rate teachers was called. People can understand that, just as they understand a shortage of nurses. But, again, we have to appreciate that there are all sorts of less obvious needs, and women can make contributions in various and quite varied ways.

I latch onto the economic and social waste, putting it first, because it's respectable, it's measurable, and lately all sorts of people out there in the real world have been noticing that women haven't been pulling their weight. But long before this happened I used to think about the waste from the point of view of the individual women—not so much in terms of what they could do for society, but what a waste it is for *themselves* and how much they would gain by being participating members of society. If it were taken for granted that once a woman's children were grown and no longer needed her full time, she would find a specific place for herself (whether through a job, volunteer work, or in some other way), she would put to better use the little scraps of time available during her busiest years.

As it is now, the short stretches of time she can find for herself are usually frittered away. It's true that during the peak of her motherhood, before the children go to school, when all of them need her almost every hour of the night and day, she has neither time nor energy to spend. The hour here, the half-hour there are needed simply for "relief" —a stolen nap, a few snatched moments of window-shopping, a story read while wheeling a carriage or stirring a pot. I remember a friend who said it was a treat to go to the dentist because she got to sit down.

But this period passes. It passes so gradually, it's true, that there isn't a precise day when a woman can say she has free time to spend and ask herself how to spend it. And just as expenses rise imperceptibly to meet rising income (Parkinson's second law), so chores and errands and what Marion Sanders calls self-perpetuating puttering, what Veblen called ceremonial futility increase as women grow older and their home duties lighter. If a young mother knew, however, that at some future time she would be allowed, encouraged, and expected to use her time, training, and abilities for some purpose, she would have something specific to do with her scraps of time as soon as they started to become just a little bigger and more dependable. Having a goal, a realistic yet flexible goal, would also add zest to a woman's life while she is still young, with time only for a course here, a volunteered hour there, or an hour in the library now and then.

Of course, while she is completely tied down, it's hard for a girl to believe she'll ever have time on her hands, that her house and her days will be empty, and she herself will be unneeded. Reaching the age of forty is like having triplets or winning the Irish Sweepstakes, the unlikely kind of thing that happens only to other people. Yet word could get through to her, somehow, that this might just possibly happen to her.

Another thing that's likely to happen—and this is something that has not been generally recognized—is that a lot of girls who now foresee only marriage and motherhood for themselves will, at some period in their lives, be looking for jobs. The Women's Bureau estimates that of the girls now in high school 8 out of 10—whether because of widowhood, divorce, economic need, emotional need, or psychological need—will at some period be employed. If girls and women could accept this while young, they'd have motivation to keep their skills from rusting, their minds from shrinking, and their work habits from deteriorating.

Perhaps a representative of the Women's Bureau should be invited to confront girls in high school and in college (the majority of whom want and see only motherhood ahead) and say to them: "I have news for you! You will be looking for a job some day, so give it a thought now, so that you'll be qualified for the best, most interesting kind of work of which you are capable." If someone could say it so that the girls would really believe it, this would be helpful—just as it would have been helpful if someone had brought news to the academic and career-minded girls of my generation that, chances were, we would not be pleading at the bar, saving humanity, or running a corporation in ten or fifteen years; we'd be marketing and cooking meals, raising our children and cleaning our houses.

As it is now, even the brightest young girl takes any old job that has a salary attached because it is frankly a stopgap until her future husband comes along or (for the lucky, the truly "in" girls) until her present husband finishes college or professional school. After that, she thinks, she'll never have to see the inside of an office or store again.

Worse than that, it seems to me, is what happens to the women who have followed the prescribed course of devoting themselves full-time to being wives, homemakers, and mothers and then find themselves —for one reason or another—looking for a job at the age of forty or fifty. They have to start at the bottom of the ladder. If they find themselves in the position of having to earn a living, it is wasteful and absurd, as well as unsatisfying, to plug away in a job far below one's capacities. If they don't have to earn money but are looking for worthwhile work, even volunteer organizations will use them in the lowliest assignments if their work habits and self-discipline have atrophied for lack of exercise. This is unsuitable for many and unbearable for some; and so, those who have any choice in the matter soon give up.

If girls could have the foresight to recognize at the beginning of their lives as women that this time will come—not only with hindsight, after a great deal of trial and error, disappointment, and heartbreak—they could try to look ahead, try to plan ahead, try to achieve some sort of balance between their work life and their personal life. My repeated use of the word "try" means I am well aware that one cannot see one's life stretching ahead, clearly and accurately. And as for planning, I realize that it is, in a sense, planning the unplannable. But if Herman Kahn and the Rand Corporation can think about the unthinkable, women should find that they have a lot to gain by planning the unplannable. If they had a general sort of goal, knowing perfectly well that it would be modified and that the road toward it would swerve and curve and, occasionally, backtrack, their journey would still be richer, more interesting, and more meaningful. If, further, they could accept such a life pattern, not as a makeshift, patched-up compromise, but as a complicated, intricate arrangement necessitated by the fact that they have the privilege and responsibility of being *both* mothers at home *and* women who have a place in the world outside the home, they could do the planning, the arranging (*and* the necessary *re*arranging) without resentment.

Last year in Belgium, while I was talking with some women about the problems connected with doing professional work while, at the same time, living a normal family life, one woman said something which I have thought of many times since then. This woman is a scientist, a *docent* at one of the universities, which is equal, approximately, to the rank of associate professor in America. She is the wife of a businessman, the mother of two sons—one at the university and one in medical school.

"When the boys were little," she told me, "my career, which was just beginning, could move along only very slowly since I was home a good deal then and couldn't spend as much time in the laboratory as my men colleagues. Even when my sons were older, but still young boys, and I had a chance to go to congresses and international meetings, for example—well, I just didn't go. I didn't really want to. Probably I didn't do as much research as I would have done had I been a man and concerned chiefly with my career. And so I didn't progress as much as if I'd been a man. I'm a *docent* now; I might perhaps have become a professor." She gave a shrug as if to say: "So what?" And then she spelled it out, quite beautifully I thought, by saying: "But that's all right for a woman because all the time you've had the pleasure of being a mother too."

And so, when I say that I'm content with second-string or second-level positions, I don't mean that women, because they are *women*, should be content with second best. I mean that if a woman is also going to run her home and be a wife to her husband and a mother to her children, it is a rare woman indeed who can hold down a full-time job which is on a par with her husband's, a rarer one still who can have a full-fledged career.

While I am wishing, I would like to get rid of the word "career" entirely. I've always been amused at the way the word "career" seems to go with the word "woman" whenever this general subject is being discussed. Most men (except for movie stars, boxers, and diplomats) have to be content with jobs. The reason the word "career" is so dangerous, I feel, when used freely, as it is, in connection with women is that many are left feeling that if they can't have a real "career," why bother at all?

Why bother? It isn't easy, I admit: this juggling of time, of energy, of one's very emotions. Sometimes you're frustrated in all your endeavors at once so that it's hard not to feel you've been left with the worst of both worlds. And yet I feel we have no choice. Maurice Chevalier is supposed to have confided to a friend: "Old age isn't so bad—not when you consider the alternative."

In much the same spirit I seriously propose that the alternative to living a full, perhaps overfull life is being half-dead. And things being the way they are, women are more likely to become victims than men. As long ago as the turn of the century Justice Oliver Wendell Holmes' wife remarked that "Washington is full of interesting men; and the women they married when they were young." This remark was sad then, but it is sadder still today, for modern couples expect more of one another in the way of companionship. We do so for a host of reasons, but one of them has to do with sheer numbers. When you look at the picture on the cover of this conference announcement, a photograph of an old-fashioned family, it's hard to tell who's the mother, who's the father, who's the husband, who's the wife. Somewhere in that large and varied group, I can't help feeling, each man and each woman could surely find a congenial soul. Today, with families small and, furthermore, isolated from grandparents, in-laws, uncles, aunts, cousins, and grown brothers and sisters, an extra demand of understanding and companionship is asked of each husband and each wife—a shared growing and deepening far beyond "developing some interests so as not to bore Jim."

Husbands, particularly, are often asked to carry an extra burden when wives expect them to supply, through their work, not only the family's entire financial support but everything that makes life "interesting." Whether they mean friends, colleagues, prestige, or being in the know depends upon each woman and what is important to her, but there are a great many who live vicariously; there are a great many young ones, newly married, who plan and expect to live vicariously, to have their husband's contact with the world make up for the fact that they have none. This, I maintain, is too much to ask of a man. And so, for the sake of the marriage, if for no other reason, each woman should continue to grow with her husband, to enrich their shared life. Mostly, however, for her own sake should she live to the full and savor to the full her "long intense alliance with the world."

Reference

1. Agnes E. Meyer, "Women Aren't Men," *The Atlantic Monthly*, 186: 32–6, August, 1950. From *Out of These Roots* by Agnes E. Meyer, Copyright 1950 by Agnes E. Meyer, reprinted by permission of Atlantic-Little, Brown and Company, publishers.

COMPETITION BETWEEN GENERATIONS

Moderator: David Krech

Dr. Krech, a founder of the Society for the Psychological Study of Social Issues, works in the fields of social psychology and the physiological foundations of behavior. He is the coauthor of a recent work, Individual in Society.

Panel Members: Lester A. Kirkendall, Hilda Sidney Krech, Russel V. Lee

Dr. Krech I must say to Dr. Kirkendall that I am a little bit upset by his discussion, because I am a lifelong opponent of sex education. I don't think there should be lecture courses in sex; there is nothing that can ruin good, unhealthy, exciting sex like a sterile lecture course.

However, Dr. Kirkendall was in favor of sex, and, as a matter of fact, he came out forthrightly for masturbation. I agree with that; however, perhaps we can get Dr. Kirkendall to come out foresquare for extramarital sexual intercourse, too. Masturbation isn't the important question when one discusses the survival of family life; the important question is something much more interesting than masturbation: it is sexual intercourse, usually between two people of different sexes outside of the marriage bounds. Are you in favor of that, and why or why not?

Dr. Kirkendall This question is not one to be passed off by a flippant comment, for I think that we are all aware that at the present time there is a tremendous public debate over what should be our moral standards. I am quite aware that what I said in my paper could by

153

logic be extended into premarital and extramarital intercourse. However, this is not the point to begin our thinking. I don't feel we should make the issue, "Should there be freedom in premarital or postmarital intercourse?" I think that we don't ask the right questions in this area to really think our way through.

In 1961 I happened to be a participant at the North American Conference on Church and Family at Green Lake, Wisconsin. This brought together about 550 church leaders from the United States and Canada. After one of our sessions I walked out of the auditorium behind a couple of religious leaders and I heard one of them say, "Well, the real question that we face here in this conference is how permissive can we be?" After thinking about this I realized that this is really the framework in which we do all of our thinking: "How permissive can we be?" The more I thought about it the more I realized that we must ask the question, "How can we integrate sex into our patterns of individual and social living so that it does provide a creative, meaningful kind of experience for the people who participate in it?" I will grant, following this logic, as we study the whole area of sexuality, and the meaning of relationships and our social fabric, that we may come some place where we have an increasing capacity for the use of intercourse in nonmarital situations, but I do not want to start there. I want to start with the concern for integrating this force into a meaningful social context. I hope this isn't evading the issue.

Before asking a question of Mrs. Krech, I would like to make a comment. In her talk, she pointed out that she would be perfectly happy to have women accept second-rate or second-string part-time whatnots, as professionals, workers, typists, etc. I would suggest that in the light of the automation in the future, when work in general will be in short supply, men, too, will have to be content with second-string, part-time jobs. There just aren't enough jobs now to go around. I would like to make this suggestion: every man at this symposium is probably already engaged in a part-time job. We are not working nearly as many hours nor using as much energy as our opposite numbers would have fifty years ago.

From that point of view, the woman whom Mrs. Krech described is probably the model for the ideal man of the future. He will be like the woman Mrs. Krech described—someone who discovers a technique of withdrawing from the labor market for a certain period of time, then comes back again just for part-time second-string work. This is because the real full-time work will probably be done by some automatic gadgets.

Dr. Lee made the statement several times that man contributes more and gets less out of marriage than does woman. I will ask Mrs. Krech a simple question, "Does she agree?"

Mrs. Krech   My answer is yes. I think that is one reason there are so many problems. Many women feel this way and resent their domesticity, wanting to go out and do things. As young women, when their husbands come home they want to know "With whom did you have lunch today?" The husbands are supposed to supply everything, interest as well as salary. This becomes more pronounced when the children are older, which reminds me of a cartoon I saw in *The New Yorker* of the poor man who comes home and whose wife says, "There you were in a nice cool sewer all day while I have been bending over the hot stove."

I don't know who works harder or has the more difficult role, but in contributing to marriage I think that during the peak years women do contribute to the family in general. If not, they may be taking away from the marriage relationship. If they are completely devoted to the children and home, they contribute to the family at that stage, and little by little as their duties fall away, women want it that way.

Dr. Krech   Will Dr. Lee start the discussion on the competition between generations?

Dr. Lee   First I want to take off a little bit on my two colleagues. Dr. Kirkendall brought a good, refreshing thought into this matter of extramarital sexual relationships. This is the puritanical influence of our society and the terrible impact of the preoccupation with peculiar manifestations of sex that Freud seemed to have encountered in his experience, causing him to lose sight of the fundamental facts. Loving is really fun and the Greek pagan idea is beginning to have some mention. While it is improper to ask anybody here as to the propriety of this, it is important not to say *what should be* but to take a look at *what is*. I am certain that such mundane considerations as improved techniques of birth control and particularly the better hygienic state that we are in now has a profound influence on how people behave.

I recall vividly the first time I ever used penicillin. I was delegated to the treatment of gonorrhea in flying personnel. Pilots were always getting that disease and would be incapacitated for six weeks. We needed fliers very badly, so all the penicillin in the Air Force was used for these cases. A young captain came in, we gave him a shot of penicillin, and in twenty-four hours he was completely cured. He came back then and we said, "You're going back to duty, you are completely well." "Gosh," he said, "it ain't no sin anymore." That is a point of view many of them had, and the very existence of venereal diseases is a reproach on the way we manage our own affairs. If you would give me 100 million dollars and less authority than Hershey had in the draft, I could guarantee that in two years there would never be another case of syphilis or gonorrhea in the United States.

The elimination of venereal disease and the development of absolutely reliable birth control methods are going to markedly change practice regardless of what you think of the propriety or whether it should be or not. There is no question but that the situation will be quite different with these two factors under control.

Coming back to the competition between generations, I am again going to take a crack at the Freudian business. All this stuff about the Oedipus complex and father murder and mother love (in a different sense than mother love is usually considered) has gotten mixed up in this generation. To feel that every son actually is the potential murderer of his father, even if he does not get around to it, is rather nonsense.

In our long history there has been cooperation between the generations much more commonly than competition. I have four sons who are doctors, who certainly compete, and a daughter who is married to a doctor, too. They are better doctors than I am, which doesn't bother me.

My son recently went to Washington for a year, and a lot of his patients came to me and said, "Dr. Phil said you would look after us when he left. We are very appreciative that you will take care of us." And then they would look at me balefully for a minute and say, "God, I wish Phil were back." That doesn't bother me at all: I rather enjoy it, as a matter of fact. I say, "Except for me he would not exist"—from which I get a lot of satisfaction. So this matter of competition between the generations is not a very real thing. There is a certain amount of parental humiliation in those areas where the boys get to be too good. Where they are better at everything than their fathers, they become contemptuous. When the automobile first came the kids learned to drive before the parents did, and other things of that kind introduced a certain amount of competition. Brokers usually bring up their children into the financial bank or stock-and-bond business. Farmers are going out of existence, so the old pattern of the boys entering into the farm is disappearing; but where farms remain they are almost all hereditary and a very satisfactory arrangement comes about. I take a rather optimistic view.

I also see very little menace in the competition between the sexes. A lot of it has been the result of certain Freudian fantasies which have no factual basis in the kind of people I see.

Dr. Kirkendall   I wanted to follow up briefly on the comment Dr. Lee made of the competition between generations. I have both a son and daughter, so I have seen some of the things he has spoken about, but I think this can be interpreted in another way: that frequently what is happening is not so much competition as it is a kind of a head-on conflict between people at different stages in their lives, each of whom is trying to accomplish certain developmental tasks necessary to his particular stage of life; and without recognition of this, trouble must ensue. Parents are always saying about their children, "Of course, they're just in that stage when . . ."—but the parents are also in similar stages. When my son who is now twenty-one attempts to be Carl Kirkendall in his own right, instead of Dr. Kirkendall's son, and makes efforts to do so, he will challenge me. He says to me, "Well, daddy, when I get big I am going to teach your classes," and my developmental task is to step out of his way. If I persist in hanging on and saying that I am indispensable, either he or some other child born in his age is going to put me out of the way. So this competition is often made worse because we're not able to mature ourselves enough to accept our stage in the life cycle and work at our developmental tasks.

Mrs. Krech   I agree. I don't think it is always competition in the Freudian sense. I don't think boys really want to kill their fathers, but they do want to feel that they are going to become somebody too, as if there were an implied competition forced on them from the outside. As you pointed out, other people continue to see Carl as Lee Kirkendall's son. Recently there was an article about me in an Oakland paper. The woman who interviewed me asked, "What is your son interested in?"

He is going on seventeen. I was not going to give her a long history of that age, so I said, "What he is interested in at the moment is social problems." So she wrote, "Her son, seventeen, is interested in social problems, which is suitable for the son of Professor David Krech, co-founder of the Society for the Psychological Study of Social Issues." This came out last Sunday and my husband was away. Two 20-year-olds were at the house and Rick was reading the article out loud. When he came to that point one of the other boys said, "Doesn't that make you want to burn down the lab?"

Dr. Krech I have taken an easy way out in order to avoid this competition between the generations. I picked a profession which no sensible, intelligent son of mine would think to follow; he is not threatening to take over my classes or my patients.

Mrs. Krech But he discovered social problems.

Dr. Krech Which suggests something you might want to discuss: how much of this competition does not exist between the generations but exists in the minds of the sociologists or psychologists who are out to observe the competition? I don't think that competition between Rick and me exists; he doesn't want to be a psychologist, for heaven sakes; but apparently it existed in the mind of that newspaper writer. How much of the competition between the generations is in the mind of the perceiver?

Dr. Lee I would say this is its chief existence. I said earlier that this stemmed, I thought, from the Oedipus concept that the Freudians stress so much, and that actually you observe any real competition between the generations very seldom.

Dr. Kirkendall I think that the extent to which this competition does exist may be a product in part of the extent to which parents and other adults feel it does. I believe this has become more diffuse and is not directed so much now to the parental role as it is to all adults. I think it is a product in part of the extent to which we disillusionize ourselves so that our young people can see us as genuine human beings.

I often tell the young people I work with that one of the problems is that they meet their parents too late in their parents' lives. Consequently they see them only as middle-aged, stodgy people who shuffle papers around on desks, and can never believe that they once were young and went through the kind of experiences that young people are going through now. Did you ever have your children find one of your baby pictures and notice the amusement they get out of it? This is because they are reconceptualizing their parents. I think that if we could make ourselves more human and relate ourselves more to our young people, a lot of difficulty would disappear.

Mrs. Krech There probably has always been competition within families. What used to be the battle of the sexes, which is not the battle that I am concerned with, is not any longer a battle between the sexes but a battle within each woman as she tries to find her place. Kids are also battling to find their places and probably always have done so, though it is supposed to be harder today without clear ideas in their minds of what they might contribute in the places they can find for themselves in the world. As Dr. Kirkendall said, the contest is not specifically with their fathers but rather with the question, can they ever be men, finding their way in a man's world?

Dr. Lee There is a point to support the idea of this competition confirmed by historical research. It is shocking how many crown princes killed their fathers to get the throne, or arranged this with associates. It still seems to be going on occasionally today. This happened at a very high level of society throughout history. Certainly it occurred all the time in Egypt, and in ancient Greek history. So I guess there is some historical background for thinking there is some competition in situations of this kind.

Dr. Krech Aren't you getting closer to the Oedipus situation?

Mrs. Krech They only disagreed with what they were fighting for, whether it was the throne or the queen.

Dr. Kirkendall I have here several written questions from the floor relating to points of view in regard to premarital intercourse and the effects of changing mores, which I consider quite fundamental.

One of the questions says, for example, "What is the effect of the birth control pills?"

I believe we must go further back and recognize that we have moved into a social situation in which our approach to moral thinking in many different areas has to be a different one. We have tended to build or rest our moral standards upon several different props which have been eroded, such as the fear-evoking deterrents of pregnancy and venereal disease, the need for using sex in the service of procreation, and now overpopulation. Science always moves in the direction of removing threats, of making the unknown known, and of helping us to manage that which has been unmanageable. This has certainly happened in the areas of reproduction and sex. We simply must invoke a different kind of thinking than we have previously. The question we must ask now is not how permissive can we be, because we have been removing these threats, but how can we integrate and incorporate these capacities into a positive, affirming life? I can see us coming to the place where there is more openness, acceptance, and ability to use nonmarital intercourse in some of our relationships.

Mrs. Krech I have been asked, "Is this problem only of modern women from your research? What was the mental attitude of woman before all this talk of the last thirty years? Were they all happy and fulfilled?"

All I know is that when I talk about the old-fashioned family and say that things are not what they used to be, my husband tells me things never were. There are two thoughts I have on the subject of happiness and fulfillment. First of all, I am sure they were not all happy. It is true that we do have higher expectations of human happiness today. Marriages are not arranged; people don't think of marriage as merely a nice social institution. They are supposed to be seeking happiness and they expect it, perhaps too much, putting too much of a strain on marriage. Every girl is going to wake up each morning and ask herself, "Am I happy, am I fulfilled?" Perhaps once the step is taken, she can realize that all unhappiness is not going to disappear, and can carry on from there. But we do expect more, and particularly women expect more than women did in the past. I don't know whether they sat around and thought about being fulfilled as such, but there were more specific things that they were supposed to do. The introverts did brood, write books, and rebel, but most women were kept too busy. There wasn't this kind of conflict because there was a tradition. A lot of women with executive ability had big organizations in the family itself, and if the grandchildren were living nearby, she could just keep on all her life. But she didn't ask herself, "What am I doing?" Life moved with her more, and we must find more in our way.

There were several other questions on education for women, such as: "Should they be educated for home life and child rearing?"

Of course the answer is yes, but I am not sure that it belongs in school. I do not believe that all education takes place in school, and I am not sure that school is the place to study about family life and the techniques of homemaking. If it can be done, this is all right. But even if it is done very well, there is an irony in it. You are building up motherhood as a "career," but what is a girl supposed to think about her own mother if she can't even teach her how to hold the baby, peel a carrot, or scrub the floor. I don't think this is an academic subject.

Dr. Lee   I have been asked to expand the contention that males contribute more to marriage than females.

I think that regardless of the material contribution the male makes to marriage, he gets out of it sexual gratification, a place to live, and food.

Now on the modern scene we might as well face the fact he can get the sexual satisfaction elsewhere, and by doing a certain amount of shopping around will perhaps get a better product than he gets at home and might get it cheaper. These are the facts of life at the present time on the sexual side. As far as living quarters are concerned, most men give up a free and easy way of living, with access to a lot of good and exotic restaurants and clubs, and to other foods, when they get married; and they get somewhat less interesting surroundings than they had in their bachelor days. This is significantly sacrificed on the part of the male, but most of all the male assumes (which the woman does not really) a tremendous economic and financial responsibility when he gets married. If there are children—and there usually are these days—he is in a position where he must support this woman and these children for the rest of their lives; not only is this a moral requirement but a legal one. This is a contribution he makes to marriage, and so I would say he does contribute more on the material side. It is true the woman gives up her freedom too, but if she is prudent in her marriage she acquires a security which the man does not. The man actually acquires hazards when he gets married. There are other tremendous advantages that the male gets, but in a completely material sense he certainly contributes more than the female.

From the Floor   Comment has been made regarding man's lack of total gratification in the marriage situation, or words to that effect. With the shrinking labor market and the role of the woman assuming a second-string position there, would Mrs. Krech care to discuss how women's future roles and the housewife's future roles could develop to fill these lacks which technology is going to produce increasingly in our economy?

Mrs. Krech As my husband so well said, we will soon be in the position where men will have half-time to work on this problem, too. Everybody knows that woman has an important function; the extra time men have can be spent in working out a better economic and social order, and we will do it together with them. This is too important for either women or men to do alone.

From the Floor Mrs. Krech, aren't you ignoring the reason for the conflict of women when you ignore the absence of such institutions as equal pay for equal work for women, free or inexpensive child-care centers, full pay with maternity leave, and full fringe benefits for part-time work?

Mrs. Krech Certainly I am for those things, as we all are. I would make two points, however. When people think it is a matter of discrimination it is not always so. For example, medical, professional, and law schools are not as quick to take equally bright girl applicants. They are entitled to think, "Is this person going to use in some way an education which so many people want?" Even if there were no discrimination there, and we had all the benefits that there should be with equal pay for equal work, there still would be an intrinsic problem. In Belgium the government gives support and tax benefits for the working woman, encouraging her in this activity. A Belgian woman said she had no conflicts of society frowning on her and it was taken for granted that she would do what she could. Even if things were right, there is an intrinsic problem that I don't think we should think of as an unfair burden. This is the way it is, and I think we can be positive. We need to be as fair as possible and work things out within the framework that we have.

Dr. Krech May I just add one comment: I don't think that I have been frustrated by anyone as much as by my women graduate students. More times than I care to count, I would get very brilliant women graduate students who were good and personable ones, dedicated to research. We would give them our all (and it is a terribly expensive and difficult job to train a good graduate student in research), and within four or five years and sometimes much sooner these women had left the laboratory after completing their Ph.D.s. I don't know whether this was always forever, but certainly they had left.

If, therefore, one has a choice between taking on a man and a woman, and all other things are equal, what can one do? There are a finite number of laboratory spaces, and in a graduate school one wants to train those who are going to carry on. Everyone who has worked either in medical schools or the sciences, and probably in every other enterprise, must recognize that even the superior woman is less likely to continue her career than a man. I am not suggesting that we develop some sort of a second-string Ph.D. degree for women so they can be second-string Ph.D. researchers later on, but that there certainly is a problem.

Dr. Lee That was true in the Stanford Medical School. I made a survey in 1940 of the careers of women graduates of Stanford Medical School. We would have done well if we had educated no women and given the places to men. Most of them had married and had made a career in marriage, dropping their medicine. It was almost a waste. There were a few notable exceptions. One of them made a great contribution in discovering the cause of San Joaquin Valley fever, but most of the women dropped out, and we should have given the places to men just on the statistics.

From the Floor I would like to ask Dr. Kirkendall, is it possible that there is a kind of a Biblical preview on the social work involved in his thesis that we need to reevaluate the role of sex in our society; for example, the Jewish dietary customs apparently arose from hygienic needs, then became crystallized as religious dogma, and now seem to be lapsing. Is that the sort of process you have in mind?

Dr. Kirkendall There are elements of similarity in it.

From the Floor If one adds up the percentage of the male population that is incompetent as far as marriage is concerned, it comes to 45 per cent. How much of an overlap do you think there is in the different categories?

Dr. Lee When I made the categories of homosexuals, impotents, psychotics, alcoholics, and economically incompetent people, there was a great overlap implied. For example, many of the economically incompetent are that way because they are alcoholics; many of the impotents are also psychotics or alcoholics. The true significance is very much lower than 45 per cent when you squeeze all the overlapping out of it. But it is very difficult to arrive at good figures in any of these categories. As the medical practitioner exposed to these failures, one is inclined to think it worse than it is; a bartender, only meeting the successes, may get a different concept of it.

A last question I have been asked during the symposium concerns a subject not touched on at any point: the consideration of idealistic and spiritual values. "Regarding your comments on the needs for a long tether, the hero-worship diet, are we not even to expect that man is more than a biological animal? Can we ever expect to want him to become emotionally mature?"

The whole symposium has been at a sociological, anthropological, biological, psychological, and medical level, and we have disregarded to a considerable degree anything of a spiritual or idealistic nature in considering the topic. I think it is perfectly possible to introduce this into the marriage situation, and here it is appropriate. My biggest success in family relations work has been to get people together and give them some notion of the idealistic marriage that included, in addition to physical pleasures and satisfactions, spiritual companionship and mental stimulation, so that they had all three and could raise the institution to a much higher level on that basis than it is now. This is an element that particularly scientists are inclined to disregard, and I have been as guilty as any in that respect. We might well follow the suggestion of this interrogator and take a look at the possibility that we might become something more than a biological animal. I think that our biological background determines what we have been, but we certainly can aspire and possibly achieve something at a higher level than that. I think that is not beyond the realm of possibility.

PART FOUR

PATHS TO THE FUTURE

Chairman: Donald H. McLaughlin

A distinguished mining engineer and formerly a member of the engineering faculties of the University of California and Harvard University, Dr. McLaughlin is also active in Bay Area affairs. He is a Fellow of the American Academy of Arts and Sciences.

The symposium closed with the paths to the future in family development. The first speaker discussed the psychological and philosophic groundwork for a realistic appraisal of new family functions. This was followed by a demonstration of the ways that the family has adapted itself to social change, and an optimistic prediction of its future. The third paper was devoted to one of the problem areas of living today: the older generation. The speaker showed that change rather than disintegration of relationships between older and younger members of the family was the pattern, and that nostalgia and individual cases were an important factor in current misevaluations. The final panel agreed that in many respects the family was stronger than in the past because it was functioning on a basis less governed by tradition and more by society; realization of the nature of social change was the most important contribution its members could make toward its further evolution as a valuable component in our civilization.

COMMITMENT TO DREAMS

Karl H. Pribram

> Dr. Pribram is a former member of the faculties of the
> University of Chicago and Yale University, and was
> Chairman of the Department of Neurophysiology at
> the Institute of Living before joining the Stanford
> medical faculty. He is broadly interested in the varied
> fields of neurophysiology, psychiatry, and philosophy.

Professor Parsons, an old friend, stated the situation succinctly when he said that since Mr. Burdick couldn't come you have to put up with an ugly scientist instead. You will have to bear with your disappointment, because, of course, what I will say will be different from what author Burdick would have said. However, I have chosen not to change the topic. I *will* talk about "Commitment to Dreams," but I will take the scientist's approach, the experimentalist's way. I will talk about the organization of the process of committing oneself to dreams, the structures of this process rather than the experience itself. This structural approach may be apposed to the existential in order to make the method clear.

You heard Dr. Parsons say yesterday that the family is changing and that perhaps it will evolve some new kind of order. My thesis is that it already has changed, that the new order is already here, that we must describe its structure. The problems that you have heard so much about may already be history; they may not really be the problems that beset the family today. When we can describe adequately the structure of the family as it truly exists today, the set of problems, or better, the attributes present, may look different from those already discussed. Only when we have done this can we tackle the appropriate set of basic attributes and face them with a commitment to dreams, not just a commitment to therapy.

The old-fashioned family of our immediate past, patriarchy or matriarchy, was organized into what I would like to call a "single-focus hierarchy." Today's family, though different, is not simply a disorganized single-focus hierarchy, as some would have us believe. Rather, its structure could be termed a "multiple-focus hierarchy." A multiple-focus hierarchy is not at all unorganized, nor unstructured. In it temporary dominances appear that govern the organization's interactions; these, in turn, are supervened by some other hierarchical organization.

This new family has evolved from the old and continues to evolve. Its attributes partake of those met in the study of evolution of any biological and therefore of any social organism or organization.

The first of these is to achieve stability. Stabilities in complex and changing systems can be achieved through any mechanism which is composed of two or more processes in reciprocal alternating communication with each other. Such a mechanism goes by the name "homeostat," which is a general form of the familiar thermostat. Biological systems built of many such devices become self-regulating and stable in the face of changes in their environment. I won't go into the details of the operation of homeostats to produce stability; you have to take my word for it that processes are stabilized by such a mechanism, and, of course, you have seen their operation yourself in the thermostatic regulation of temperature.

In addition to stability, two other attributes emerge when biological or social systems evolve: differentiation and change. In today's context, differentiation is the attribute which leads to the formation of dreams, and change is the one which results in commitment.

Let me illustrate with a simple experiment.

(*He hits the desk with a hard piece of wood.*) Most of you reacted to this sudden sound by measurable physiological and behavioral changes which together are known as the orienting reaction. Some of you started, some of you turned toward the sound. The electrical activity in your brains changed. This is called the alerting reaction. The electrical resistance of your skin took a sharp dip, and there was probably a slight shift in the distribution of your blood—less in the finger-tips, more to the brain.

(*He hits the desk repeatedly.*) Less and less do you react. This is called habituation, and for a long time we believed that habituation resulted when our nervous systems, our reactive systems, became *less* sensitive when repeatedly exposed to the same input—in this case the sound. Eugene Sokolov in Moscow showed this view to be in error through the following experiment: He habituated a person to a sound just in the way I did with you a moment ago; then he *decreased* the intensity of the sound. Immediately the person again showed the orient-ing reaction; all the same physiological indexes of orienting, alerting returned. Sokolov reasoned from this that the sensitivity of the nervous system could not be decreased during habituation. He tested his reason-ing by experiment: He again habituated his subject and then *shortened* the duration of the stimulus. Again his subject oriented, but this time the orienting reaction was not to the sound but to the *silence*.

This fundamental experiment shows that through our experiences with our environment some model of this environment is built up in our brains. Another way of stating this is to say that we continually come to our environment with a model or expectation of what it will be like. This model or expectancy turns out to be very precise, and we alert, orient whenever any slightest deviation from the expected is experienced.

Differentiation takes place in a homeostatic system by virtue of these expectancies. Let me illustrate. Originally thermostats were crude. They helped turn on the furnace in the morning and that was a boon: we didn't have to go down at five o'clock in the morning to stoke the furnace. Just for the thermostat to accomplish that much and not to allow the fire to go out was already a tremendous help. But thermostats improved and one day people began to notice that around dinner time, around dusk, the house became cold and uncomfortable. They would go to their thermostat and see that it was still set at 70 degrees, just as it had been an hour before when the sun was shining and the house was comfortable. But now it was uncomfortable. Even after drafts were eliminated mother shuddered when she sat down to supper and said, "It is chilly in here. I wonder if you left the window open." Of course, there was no draft, no window open. The outside walls of the house had become cooled and the radiation from the body to the walls accounted for these chilly feelings. As a result of its perfected stability the system had precise "expectations" which allowed for new sensitivities. The solution to this problem was, of course, to add another thermostat on the outside wall and to connect it to the first one to help modulate the regulatory functions of the first thermostat. Instead of a single-focus regulation, a dual-focus control system was now operating.

As our society became still more affluent, people began to demand different temperatures in the bedroom and different temperatures at different times of the day. So, a third thermostat and timing devices were added to the system. It has truly been differentiated into a multi-focus control system. When stability was accomplished, precise expectancies could be achieved through habituation, and new sensitivities thus allowed to develop.

Dreams—and I am not talking, of course, about the dreams one has when one is asleep but those one lives when one is awake—are developed in the same way. In the presence of a certain amount of equanimity, habituation to the environment proceeds to build up precise expectancies, dreams of what should or could be. These are fashioned, differentiated from the family or work situation in much the same way as our sensitivities to cold in a thermostatically controlled home. And we devise new ways to cope with these new sensitivities.

Let me give you another example, but this one is more biological. When the human organism first is born, he is very dependent on his environment, especially on his social environment, his mother. At first he considers himself and his mother to be a unitary system. After a while, it becomes evident to him that his mother and he are two separately controlled systems—he can function, in some situations, independently. After this initial differentiation which has so often been described, after the infant has differentiated between his mother and himself, he begins to realize that all the things that his mother usually does, such as feed him, are occasionally not performed by her. Once in a while his father will come in with a glass of milk or a bottle, and a new differentiation is made. Feeding is a system in itself and may be participated in by individuals other than his mother (and even himself), and this system in itself becomes regulated. A system of roles is formed. But the preconditions for role formation are seen to be stability and the development of precise expectancies—only then can the sensitivities to what we label role be established. Our dreams are akin to the system of roles. The dreamer dreams his role in a projected universe.

And so we come finally to the most difficult part of this mechanism: how the attribute of commitmènt emerges. Given the fact that differentiation will take place, that people will dream, we now ask, how do they become committed to the dream? How do they change the stable order so that they actually do something about what hitherto had been only seen at first dimly and then clearly—differentiated out as walls becoming cold at dusk, as fathers feeding in lieu of mothers. What seems to happen is that the inputs which hitherto had been providing information to the system in its search for what was making it sensitive suddenly—and this usually takes place dramatically—become organized not only as expectations but into the antecedents of action. The organism apparently reverses "the tape recording" and plays through all that he has been building up but, in a sense, backward— and I mean this quite literally with regard to how the nervous system operates during this reversal. We are just beginning to program computers to do this sort of thing: a discrimination tree is built up through a program and then reversed when, for example, equivalences are called for. My suggestion is that it is this rather dramatic reversal that is at the basis of what we feel when we become committed. Whenever this happens, what was information before now values our performances. We are no longer differentiating roles, building expectations, dreaming dreams. We are now taking roles, planning on the basis of our expectations, living the dream.

Now if this is indeed the threefold process by which commitment to dreams is achieved, we have learned a great deal about the family of today. First, stabilities must be ensured; then differentiations will take place by virtue of the expectations that develop from these stabilities; and finally reversal, i.e., commitment, follows. Given internal stability and a rich external environment this family process should develop as assuredly as that of biological evolution.

As long as we had a single-focus family hierarchy there was no problem. Stability was assured and a single differentiated "tree" developed. Each time a reversal took place it originated at the top. Decisions were made, commitments undertaken by the head of the family; others participated in this commitment. The dream was clear; there was only one commitment to be made. But families today are organized in another way. There are several possible foci of control around which the family system can stabilize, and these interact and interrelate. Sometimes one and sometimes another member of the family, sometimes another role, sometimes one dream, sometimes another become the dominant one guiding the family. Therefore commitment may be postponed, since no single focus ever dominates sufficiently long or sufficiently strongly to allow differentiation and reversal to occur.

This then is our problem: to study the development of multifocus hierarchies and to locate the differences and similarities in the processes by which they attain maturity. Only then will we be able to ascertain how systems such as the modern family and the individuals that compose it can make their commitment to dreams. This much can be learned from the structural approach to the process of commitment. We have a way of describing what must be taking place in the current family which, contrary to some opinions, is not disorganized but has a multiple-focus type of structure. What we must now study are the attributes and thus the problems faced by a multiple-control system, one that is not pyramidally organized. This can be accomplished by the aid of simulation on computers, and we should learn a great deal this way in the next few years.

Finally, let me state that the particular view and approach that I have taken here is, of course, only one of several that would be of use. I have talked about structure; I have not talked about the events within the structure. I have talked of thermostatic systems, not of furnaces or fuel; of roles, not persons. But to talk of heat and people only also limits severely what we must understand. The structural approach to family process is effective, as already shown by the work of Drs. Don Jackson and Gregory Bateson, and their collaborators in Palo Alto.

And so the phenomenon of commitment to dreams, although an issue which has until now been thought to be purely the province of existential psychology and psychiatry, can be illuminated considerably by taking the structural approach. Dreams and commitments thus become not nebulous hopes despairing and defying treatment when they become problems, but scientific issues that can be examined and successfully operated upon.

THE FAMILY AND SOCIAL CHANGE:
A POSITIVE VIEW

Judson T. Landis

An author and investigator in the field of family relations, Dr. Landis is also a Research Associate in the Institute of Human Development, Berkeley. He is a member and past president of the National Council on Family Relations, and his recent works include Youth and Marriage *and* Marriage and the Family.

Some twenty-five years ago when I was studying people sixty-five years old and older I asked them at what period in life they had been happiest and why they had been happiest at that time. By far the largest percentage said they were happiest during the period after marriage and before their children had left home. The things they most often mentioned as bringing greatest happiness had to do with marriage and parenthood.

Last year a study was made of over 2,000 alumni of a West Coast liberal arts college to determine what had brought greatest personal satisfaction to these college graduates as adults. By far the most common thing mentioned was family relationships. For both men and women career or occupation ran a poor second to the family in bringing personal satisfaction to them.

I mention these studies because I think at times we tend to lose perspective on life values and satisfactions. We focus only upon the shortcomings of family life in America: divorce, delinquency, illegitimacy, alcoholism, suicide, murders, mental breakdowns. It is easy to think that relatively few people find their satisfactions within the family framework, or that there are few happy marriages. And yet research with American families shows that the majority of married couples consider their marriages to be happy. And even though we have in California the highest divorce rate of any state and in the United States one of the highest divorce rates in the world, there is no indication that people are disillusioned with the institution of marriage. A larger percentage of the population of the United States marries today than ever before in our history: 92 out of 100 people will eventually marry. People who fail in one marriage are not turned against marriage but are more likely to remarry than are single people of the same age to marry. Young people are marrying at an earlier age and are starting their families at a younger age than has been true in past generations. The rush to early marriage and parenthood is a symptom of family failure, youth grasping for security they have not found in their own homes. I think the family of the future can function more positively than has the family in the past if conscious effort is made today to understand the changes taking place in the family and if young people are prepared to understand what they undertake when they marry. Those who think we should go back to the good old days—when there were few or no divorces—should not look too closely at the family as it was in the past.

Let me list briefly some of the changes that have taken place in the family; many of these have been explored most interestingly in this conference. In the past in our country (and it is still the case in most countries of the world today), marriages were arranged by the parental families to protect the social, economic, and political interests of the two families concerned. Happiness and companionship were not considered important in arranging a marriage. The arranged marriage protected family interests and provided for heirs to carry on the family, generation after generation. Women and children had no legal rights; children were unplanned; sexual enjoyment was for men, not women; the husband or possibly the husband's father or mother ruled the household. The husband might have a mistress or concubines. Many societies, including our own, had a double standard of sexual morality. True, the divorce rate was very low in our country and it remains low in most countries where this system of arranged marriage prevails today. But a low divorce rate does not necessarily mean marriages are successful or happy for the individuals involved.

In the United States we have been struggling toward a different basis for marriage. We have set up goals of happiness, companionship, fulfillment of individual needs, legal equality, a single standard of sexual morality, and democracy within the family. These are difficult goals to achieve. Young people in other countries who have been exposed to the idea of what they call "love" marriages in the United States are highly favorable to the idea. In most countries of the world today there is a breaking away from arranged marriages as educated young people are attempting to copy what they understand as the American way in family life. We could become concerned about other countries copying our marriage system when we can see so many defects in the way our system works. Those who feel that a low divorce rate is a reliable index of family success might even make a good case for our copying the arranged family system of the Orient.

In this conference we have had some dialogue about whether we are pessimists or optimists as we look at the American family. I don't know how I would be classified on that. Perhaps I am a pessimist with an optimistic outlook. It seems to me good that the movement is toward recognizing the family's basic functions to be meeting deep adult needs and providing a climate for healthy personality growth of children. And I am encouraged about the family's future when I see the concern and contributions made by so many different disciplines as represented in this conference. Problems of the family must be approached from all possible directions. Law, medicine, sociology, psychiatry, and many other fields—each with its own approach—ought to be worth something to American families.

For many American families *are* in trouble; many of them are failing in their basic functions. In view of the courtship and marriage system today, what can be done to help the family achieve its function of providing individual fulfillment for all members?

First, we ourselves must see marriage and help young people to see it, realistically, as a way of life that requires more of the individual than single living does. Married living requires a level of cooperation and flexibility that is seldom required of the single person. This fact is not acknowledged in the popularly accepted romantic view of marriage in our society. Yet every person who makes a success of marriage knows it to be true. In our society we seem to maintain a conspiracy of silence on such matters. The norm is marriage and parenthood. People are pressured to conform to that norm. Mass media and all kinds of advertising push people toward conformity. Every person must fall in love, marry, and have children. Without debating the statistics Dr. Lee gave, I would agree that a great many people, both men and women, should never marry, and many of those who do marry should never have children. Many people who may possibly cope with a relationship with a husband or wife still cannot be adequate parents. Ninety-two out of one hundred people marry, but certainly not that high a percentage *should* marry.

Half of American girls are married by the time they are twenty and half of the boys before they are twenty-three. More girls marry at age eighteen than at any other age. Choosing the right marriage partner is more closely associated with successful functioning in life than any other decision the individual makes, yet in our society the majority of girls and a large percentage of boys make this decision before we consider them old enough to vote. The trend toward earlier marriage, which grows out of the trend toward earlier dating, is a serious hazard to family life in America. Many studies have been made relating age at marriage to divorce and to happiness in marriage, and without exception the studies show that teen-age marriages are much more likely to end in divorce or to be unhappy even if they remain intact. Those of us who have worked closely with failing families know that much of the failure in marriage is due to failure *before* marriage. If the best path to a good marriage is for individuals to choose their own mates, more must be done in a positive way to guide youth in making choices. There must be more careful preparation for marriage and parenthood.

Few young people are really mature enough for marriage and parenthood before they reach their twenties. Our society has encouraged youth in a rush toward a pseudo-maturity. Instead of there being a carefree period of youth between childhood and adulthood, people today rush from childhood to experiences that require more maturity than can be achieved so fast. Dating in grade school, steady dating in junior and senior high school, marriage at graduation from high school, and two or three children by the age of twenty-one is not a sound procedure for the average person. Those marrying in their teens are as a group the less mature; certainly many of them will not be emotionally mature enough for parenthood until long after they have had their last child. We are actually faced with the problem of child marriages and child parenthood. In 1960 there were 600,000 children born to teen-age mothers. A generation ago two-thirds of divorcing couples in the United States had no children because having children was postponed for a few years after marriage, but today two-thirds of divorcing couples have children, since parenthood now is begun early in marriage. The fact that more girls are going through divorce between the ages of twenty and twenty-five than at any other five-year period in life suggests that there should be a slowing up in the rush to take on the responsibilities of marriage and parenthood. The family of the future can be strengthened through educating the young to approach marriage cautiously, and through arming them with realistic information about marriage and parenthood.

When I speak of education for marriage and parenthood I mean specific units and courses at different grade levels in the public schools which give accurate information on the realities of marriage and parenthood. Much of what our young people believe about marriage is fiction. Rather than being cautious about entering marriage, they tend to think that marriage can be an escape from personal or parental problems. Teen-age songs, movies, and much of the writing in current magazines do not give an accurate picture of marriage. Family life education in the schools should include discussions of danger signals in courtship which should warn youth against making marriages which cannot possibly work. It should face the difficulties of continuing an education while married, consider the economic aspects of married living, the maturity necessary to make the many adjustments required in marriage, and the physical and emotional energy needed to be a good parent. My experience in working with university students has convinced me that our greatest hope in building a stronger family life is in educating people before they marry or become parents and before they are confronted with problems and frustrations which may block their learning processes. In fact, the education must come *before* they are involved in choosing a mate. In courses in preparation for marriage for university students I am constantly thinking of these students' children who are not yet born. Helping the family achieve a higher level of success and cutting down the social wastage from family failure is not a short-term project. In the past we have tended to build hospitals at the bottom of the cliff to care for those who fall from the mountain, rather than to build barriers at the top so that fewer will fall. It is time that we engaged in an active preventive program so that more marriages and families may succeed in rearing marriageable children.

Second, society must continue to expand its services to families in need. Family problems, whether between husband and wife, or special problems with children are the concern of society. Almost all studies of the growth and development of children and of the functioning of adults in society show that there is a close relationship between the individual's functioning in society and the quality of the relationships within his family. The evidence is so overwhelming now that we have come to think of "sick" families, "failing" families, or families living in an emotionally unhealthy climate. In treating individual members of the family it must be more generally known that the whole family is involved in emotional or mental disorders of the individual. Statistical studies of delinquency, crime, suicide, and neuroses show that all these indices of failure are closely associated with failure in family living. Similarly, studies show that those who are able to establish happy homes, develop competence in handling their personal problems, and cope with crises in life are more likely to come from successful families. It is realistic for society to accept responsibility for helping troubled families.

Evidence of the fact that families pass on success and failure is found in the history of divorce in families. I am interested not in divorce per se but in what it represents. The findings of research on divorce mean that successive generations of some families fail to meet the personality needs of the adults or to provide an environment for healthy personality growth of children. I collected the family histories of 2,000 students at the University, obtaining marital histories of the grandparents, parents, and aunts and uncles. The study revealed that if neither set of grandparents had divorced, only 15 per cent of their children had divorced; if one set of grandparents had divorced, 24 per cent of their children had divorced; but if both sets of grandparents had divorced, 38 per cent of their children had divorced [1]. Other studies have shown a very close relationship between the failure of parents in marriage and failure of their children in marriage. And we should note again here that divorce is not a very accurate measure of the success or failure of families. It is used because it is one objective criterion that does give some light on failure. A recent study emphasizes this point for me. In studying the maturation of 3,000 students, I found that those from unhappy homes had received about the same adverse conditionings as had those from divorced homes. In some respects those who had been reared in unhappy but unbroken homes had received more handicaps. Those young people who had grown up in happy homes had a higher conception of self in that they had greater confidence in their ability to make successful marriages, they had less difficulty in making friends with the other sex, and in general they placed a higher evaluation upon themselves and their ability to cope with life [2].

Failing families need help to end the cycle of failure in successive generations. The attack must be waged on many fronts. There must be more adequate and available marriage counseling for couples in trouble, family clinics for families with child problems, school counselors trained to recognize and assist children who are headed for trouble. There must be more adequate psychiatric services for the seriously disturbed at every age level. All of these are needed for disturbed families; we can hope that the proportion of emotionally crippled families will decrease as our marriage education becomes more effective.

Third, we must accept the fact that even at best some marriages fail and divorce becomes necessary. If we can be rational rather than emotional, we know that many couples should divorce, both for their own sake and for the sake of their unborn children. Nevertheless there should be a complete revision of our divorce procedure. Family courts should be established, and rather than the philosophy being one of sin, guilt, and recrimination the criterion would be what is best for the family. People should be able to turn to the family court when they are in trouble. It would be the job of the family court to have trained counselors to counsel and study the family and make recommendations to the court as to what future course the family should follow. In some cases the recommendation would be for the family to be dissolved [3].

Recently I completed a study of 330 university students, all of whom were children of divorced parents. An attempt was made to study the trauma of children in divorce from the child's point of view. There is not time to go into the research here other than to point out this finding: chronically unhappy couples who are in constant conflict might better divorce for the sake of the children. The research showed that there were cases in which the children were on the way to emotional recovery with a termination of the unhappy marriage. The research also showed another type of case in which the child thought everything was fine until suddenly the parents decided to divorce. In these cases it is not the unhappy home that is traumatic for the child but the divorce and the adjustment to divorce. If we had adequate counseling services for families, and if we had predivorce counseling, couples could be helped to know whether theirs is a marriage that should end for the sake of the children or whether it is one which should be preserved for the sake of the children. Couples themselves are often not in a position to know. Counseling with those divorcing could also help the people know whether they are unmarriageable or whether a second marriage might possibly work [4].

Basic to all programs devoted to aiding families to achieve their greatest potential in the future is a strong program of research on all aspects of family life. Research information is now available on the family background situations and on the personality characteristics which make individuals marriageable. Research findings are providing more insight into danger signals in courtship which should warn youth against making marriages which cannot possibly work [5]. Several studies of marital adjustment show what are the universal problems which couples face as they try to learn to understand each other during the first years of marriage. For example, a kind of knowledge now available through research is a picture of the patterns of adjustment in the early years of marriage. Research shows that the adjustments all couples go through tend to fall into rather specific patterns [6]. Progress toward sound and successful relationships in a family can be charted. Certain kinds of adjustments take more time than others for most people. Such knowledge contributes to the building of better marriages.

As we look to the future we have certain choices in considering the direction of the family. First we can muddle along as at present, knowing that the family is the most important unit in society in molding the next generation, but actually doing little except making some attempts to pick up the pieces after families are wrecked. Rather than developing preventive programs, we can accept child marriages, high divorce, and illegitimacy, and continue building institutions for the emotionally disturbed.

We can refuse to face the problems of the family and talk of turning back to the past when there was a low divorce rate, when women kept their "rightful" place in the kitchen, when research on marriage was taboo, when people who could bear children were considered wise enough to rear their children and when marriage counseling and marriage education were not considered important.

I think our alternative is to redouble our efforts to help American families fulfill their function. We must increase understanding through research on all aspects of marriage and child development; we must increase help for disturbed families; we must provide economic assistance for children in underprivileged homes; we must continually improve family life education in the schools and colleges.

We hear much about the need to strengthen certain courses in the physical sciences, but in revising and strengthening educational programs we should recognize that the greatest failure today is in interpersonal relationships. Failing families are producing more emotional cripples than we can afford. In planning educational programs we must consider what is most important in educating youth for the world we hope they will survive to live in. Our educational system has already demonstrated its ability to produce scientists who can destroy the world. The educational system must now produce people with enough understanding of human relationships to prevent world destruction. Goals of happiness within the family, the meeting of individual needs, and democracy are not unrealistic. But to achieve these goals we must increase efforts in education and research. If we meet the challenge facing us, I think we can be optimistic about the family's future.

References

1. Judson T. Landis, "The Pattern of Divorce in Three Generations," *Social Forces,* 34(3):213–216, March, 1956.
2. Judson T. Landis, "Dating Maturation of Children from Happy and Unhappy Marriages," *Marriage and Family Living,* 25(3):351–353, August, 1963. Judson T. Landis, "A Comparison of Children from

Divorced and Nondivorced Unhappy Marriages," *The Family Life Coordinator*, 11(3):61–65, July, 1962.

3. Paul W. Alexander, "A Therapeutic Approach to the Problem of Divorce," *Law Forum*, 36, 1950, reprinted in Judson T. Landis and Mary G. Landis, *Readings in Marriage and the Family*, Englewood Cliffs, N.J., Prentice-Hall, Inc., 1952, p. 360.

4. Judson T. Landis, "The Trauma of Children When Parents Divorce," *Marriage and Family Living*, 22(1):7–13, February, 1960.

5. Judson T. Landis and Mary G. Landis, *Building a Successful Marriage*, 4th ed., Englewood Cliffs, N.J., Prentice-Hall, Inc., 1963, Chap. 6.

6. Judson T. Landis, "Length of Time Required to Achieve Adjustment in Marriage," *American Sociological Review*, XI(6):666–677, December, 1946.

THE INTIMATE RELATIONS
OF OLDER PEOPLE

Alvin I. Goldfarb

A noted psychoanalyst, Dr. Goldfarb holds many positions in New York City, including that of Consultant on Psychiatric Services for the Aged for the New York State Department of Mental Hygiene. He is also Chief of Neuropsychiatry at the Home for Aged and Infirm Hebrews and is a member of the Gerontological Society.

As the last on the program I have the unusual privilege of being able to comment on all of the preceding talks. As I see it, there is no question that the family will survive, but there is a question of what kind of family we will have in the future. We seem to have come a long way toward developing some good families. Will we continue to do so? Can we socially favor the formation of sound family structure or will we "slip"? I am not optimistic. However, although I have definite opinions which I am sure will shine through what I have to say, I will try, when referring to different types of socialization and the products of such socialization, not to characterize them as to value; I will try to remember to refer to them simply as "Type 1" and "Type 2."

Over forty years ago Stekel remarked that most troubled people want to be loved because "to be loved means to be understood." This brief statement about human relationships may be highly revealing of acquired human needs and human motivations. When the statement is reversed to read that to be understood is to feel loved, it reveals that, more than they want actual help, individuals want empathy and to believe they can get help if they want it. They want to feel secure in the knowledge that their needs are recognized and their burdens will be accepted. Even more, as Schnitzler put it, "To understand all is to forgive all"; thus to be loved, to be understood, is to be accepted unconditionally. This is what many older people seem to want from the people around them.

With this in mind, I would like to touch upon three seemingly unrelated topics, which, when taken together, may increase our understanding of the intimate relations of older people.

First is the problem of loneliness and boredom. These are two symptoms of troubled social relationships. They are important to a humane society which believes in preventing the development of pain and suffering and in helping those in whom it arises. Second is the attitude of families in our society toward older persons: are families or communities rejecting and neglecting, or are they helpful, tolerant, and supportive? Third is the question of residential care of the old or aged: is institutionalization of older persons to be avoided whenever feasible in favor of care in the private home, or is institutionalization to be looked upon more favorably and encouraged? I do not promise to answer all of these questions; just to talk about them.

It is clear that I have broken into several parts a popular belief which can be summarized as follows: "Many of the old or aged are lonely and bored, they lead isolated, empty lives; if ill or discouraged, they become more so; if they are not, then they become so through self-neglect, family disinterest, and lack of opportunity; moreover, they are prematurely retired, are rejected by our society; their families do not hold them in high regard, and they have no sustaining social roles; thus, when they become ill or in need of some special services, they have no place to go and, much to their chagrin and distress, they tend to end up in an institution; this adds to their pain and suffering, and because of the dislocation and further neglect, they die."

First, consider the lonely and bored aged. In recent years the loneliness and boredom of the aged have been very frequently portrayed for us in story, film, and magazine article; you will recall the lonely old man or woman disconsolate in the shabby room, or even in the luxurious house; the aged person forlornly sitting in the park or wandering down the street. Each of us is probably personally acquainted with at least one bored old person who has nothing to do, who has been relieved of household duties or retired from work, and who may well appear to be neglected by family and friends. Such people often call themselves to our attention with heart-tugging force. Most evocative of strong feelings can be the older or aged persons we meet—casually or professionally—who manage to impress us through a seemingly brave show of busyness with how bored and lonely they are and feel; they command sympathy because of how well they are carrying on despite a solitary state and a life empty of the many interests of their past.

How can we account for the plight of these persons? Why are they forlorn? What do they need? Are they socially isolated through no fault of their own, neglected by family, friends, and neighbors, asking only for the neighbor's smile, or the friendly visit; are they ready and able, were it only available, to profit from the meal on wheels or the family gathering, or to make use of the neighborhood golden-age, wagon-wheel, or senior-citizen group? Are they the rejected who, could they but live with a son or daughter, would bloom and flourish once more and, physical health permitting, become relatively active, alert, and productive members of the family or the community?

At the risk of seeming callous or cold, I would encourage looking at these people and at their problems with a somewhat clinical or jaundiced eye lest too ready an extension of pity, sympathy, or compassion interfere with our ability to offer helpful warmth and helpful effort; an unimpassioned view is necessary if we are to gather the information necessary for us to be helpful.

Loneliness and boredom, after all, are not limited to the old or the aged; they are found in persons at any age. What is it that the lonely person feels? In the sense of loneliness there appears to be a longing for the comfortable, the serene, the tender, the stimulating, the desirable, the amusing, the interested, the attentive—other person. Such longing for another, or others, can be felt even when one is in a group. It is a nostalgic experience, a yearning; it is like a hunger or a thirst; it is mixed with sadness and often with anger; it can lead to tears or rage; it may make one restless or apathetically still. The viewer may discern, and the lonely person himself may recognize, the nostalgia. Those persons with illness, impairment, or loss of ability to pursue their work or usual interests appear to feel saddened that loved ones do not rally round. However, we see that for these persons even all reasonable aid and interest from the family may not suffice. In many, the self-pitying, lonely feeling is perennial and not contingent upon any new loss of ability or opportunity, and it is never eased completely or for very long by any attention, however great—it is a chronic state that has long antedated the problems of older age. In old age the nostalgic state has merely emerged to be troublesome in a new social situation which seems to place new burdens upon bewildered family members. Thus, loneliness often reveals itself to be not a problem easily solved by family interest or answered by community clubs, but rather a symptom of depression which requires technical skills for its relief.

And so it is also with boredom. Boredom is not an inactive, empty psychological state, as it is so often described or thought to be; it is rather an active, irritated, cranky, querulous condition. It may be overtly quiet; but when it is not openly displayed, then contained within the individual is a seething unrest. Boredom is a state of being in which one is not getting what one wants when one wants it or what one needs when one needs it and, simultaneously, is not able to move out, to reach out, to get it. It is the listening to someone in whom one is not interested, and the being prevented, by politeness or fear, from saying so or leaving; it is doing what does not amuse one, or it is not doing what one would like to do, yet feeling restrained and prevented from abandoning the pursuit and going on to what one prefers.

Boredom is, in short, the effect of restricted self-assertion in the presence of tensions that call for relief. What prevents one from acting unless the desire for self-assertion is joined by anger? Perhaps we can derive some clues by defining the mentally healthy.

The mentally healthy older person has needs that do not differ greatly from those of younger persons. He desires friendships of varying types and intimacy with both sexes, and wants to keep busy at work or a play equivalent which is within his physical capacities, is commensurate with his intelligence and background of training, and from which he derives a sense of accomplishment. He looks for, and objects to frustration of, opportunities for the relief of biological tensions such as hunger and sexual desire, and for the gratification of culturally determined needs.

In addition he may crave, in varying degrees, appreciation, marks of affection, and reassurance that he has made an impression upon this world in his lifetime by means of his words or his deeds, or by having reproduced himself. These can maintain the self-esteem which in the past rested upon, and was reinforced by, his performance or his hopes. In all this there may be some differences from youth, called mellowness —a lack of haste, an inner patience, and a philosophic tolerance that grow out of a satisfied curiosity. But most important he has internalized the values of his culture so that he has been and continues to be capable of playing the various roles required by his achieved or ascribed status. He has been and is a rational, considerate, cooperative, self-reliant, self-disciplined person who can gain pleasure through his own efforts and with others.

By contrast, those who appear lonely, bored, in need of love and understanding, and make a point of it appear to have reproduced, to have been productive, and to have gained pleasure through, by means of, or for—to please—another; they have tended to serve or to control others, and in this way have held them because of their need to feel secure.

The healthy appear to have been socialized so that they internalized the values of their culture. Each has made an adequate, useful identification with a parental figure or a suitable idealized image, and has been and remains suitably self-assertive, with a capacity to maintain self-esteem through achievement or recollection of success, with self-confidence, and with a sense of purpose. We can call this person, who is nondependent, a product of "Socialization Type 1" [1].

The unhappy, discontented older persons appear to have been socialized as dependent persons who are anxious when they are, or feel they are, alone, who are prone to occasions of feelings of helplessness, and tend to devote their lives to searching for the support of others through whom they gain their sense of worth and their self-confidence. They make demands on the views of others, and they find purpose in the pursuit of others. We can call these persons products of dependent "Socialization Type 2."

The confidential conversation of the lonely and the aged confirms the impressions gained from their behavior with friends and relatives, that they are searching for a potentially protective, interested person with whom they can establish a relationship in which, however it is disguised, they feel controlling, and therefore secure. No matter what friends or family members are actually available, or how frequently they are seen, in their search for the special person the aged may complain of and experience loneliness and boredom; and even when the sustaining person is found the complaint may persist, although the subjective pain may decrease because the complaint is the means of maintaining the relationship they desire.

In their search for a protective, interested person, they generally look first to family members, which brings us to our second consideration: the attitudes of families—are they accepting or rejecting? Sociologic studies of morale, which I can roughly translate into the psychiatric term of depressive trend or depression, have provided some helpful data. It appears that the aged who see their relatives, their families with frequency have lower morale—more symptoms of depression—than those who see their families with lesser frequency. This appears to be true also for visits with friends. Are we to assume that visiting or being visited by family or friends is depressing, that the family members with whom they visit are being rejecting or neglecting? This may be true, but here clinical experience indicates that it is much more likely that need for the support, reassurance, and comforting presence of an interested other person determines both the frequency with which a family will be visited by, or will be prompted to visit, an older person. In retired persons with leisure time such needs probably determine the frequency of social contacts in general. Persons who have high morale, who are not depressed, do not pursue their families for support and are not indiscriminate in their socialization; conversely, persons in search of companionship are often anxious and demoralized.

A survey of a sample of aged persons who live in a housing project tends to bear this out: these aged persons, well enough to manage their own apartments, complained chiefly about the community in which they lived; they did not complain very much of loneliness, boredom, lack of interested relatives, or lack of frequent contact with other persons. Few of them belonged to social clubs, and most said they would not want any more social contacts than they already had. These aged persons, who lived as couples or alone, indicated what they wanted was better transportation, better and less expensive stores nearby, and good, convenient medical-care facilities; not visitors, clubs, and recreational facilities.

In addition to having less need for frequent social contact, persons with high morale are often in good health, for ill health is conducive to depression, and it is frequent for persons who are ill to need the attentions of their families constantly or intermittently. However, the rich aged have higher morale than the poor aged, and economic security or relative affluence is so potent a protection against mental depression that it can work counter to ill health. In short, from the psychiatric point of view, it seems that it is better to be rich and sick than poor and healthy. The well-off who are in good health have the highest morale, or the least severe and intractable depressions, while among the sick poor are seen the most malignant and severe. But these socioeconomic and health factors may mask some others, and the factors that are masked take us back to the importance of the socialization process.

The rich aged generally have had good early socioeconomic opportunities for the development of internal resources which tend to maintain morale, that is to say, counter the development of depression. These are, for example, formal and informal education, learning through occupational pursuits and travel; the development of interests in books, art, music, conversation, and even just thinking that can be carried into old age. The poor from early in life have been deprived, and early deprivation has precluded investments which would ensure dividends in later life. Almost as with money itself, so it is with health, and it is also with morale: "Them as has gits; them as hasn't doesn't." This seems true except for one phenomenon, which I find rather cheerless; among the relatively socioeconomically deprived there may tend to be groups in which family closeness is high, intimacy is great, and family solidarity is marked.

I find this cheerless because this closeness appears to be comprised of interlacing pain-filled personal relationships in which manipulative maneuvering is called, and mistaken for, affection, and in which guilt, a crushing sense of obligation, and a compulsive need for social compliance, joined with fear and inability to act with rational independence, combine to constitute a reciprocal bondage miscalled "love." These are persons whose great family cohesion is based upon the socialization of the family members as dependent persons whose pleasures are contingent upon their feeling that a parent surrogate is always available.

Thus it happens that family members to whom lonely and bored persons turn for aid do try to help but are limited by their own needs and by their inability to supply to the person what should actually come from within him: a capacity for pleasure and an ability to take pride in himself. Their assistance must fall short of the aged person's needs, except in so far as they meet his need to find purpose in courting them and pleasure in winning their interest, and from the sense of strength gained in controlling them.

In Table 1, I have charted some of the factors which appear to contribute to high morale—that are counterdepressants. We see that with relative affluence the individual has economic security and physical security, which have the protective effect of permitting him to feel rela-

Table 1   Contributors to "high morale," counterdepressive factors

Factor	Protective device	Protective effect	Result
Relative affluence	Economic security: food, shelter, services, mobility, medical care Physical security: power, physical comfort or pleasure	Freedom from fear and anger Assertiveness	Limited need for family and friends
High educational level	Well-established mechanisms of psychological, social, and emotional adjustment Diversity and range of interests	Self-confidence Self-esteem Self-direction: interests, purpose Sense of identity	Responsiveness to need of family Capacity for solitary self-enjoyment
Social status	Social security	Social independence	Ability for independent productive or pleasurable activity
Good health	Power Mobility Physical comfort or pleasure Physical security	Physical independence	

tively free from fear and anger, and free to be assertive so that he has limited need for family and friends. Similarly, with a high educational level he can be expected to have well-established mechanisms of effective psychological, social, and emotional adjustment; this is analogous if not identical with what Dr. Krogman called politeness—this will be well-automatized and the individual will have self-confidence, self-esteem, purposefulness, and a sense of identity which makes him responsive to the needs of his family and capable of relatively solitary self-enjoyment and so on down the line of this somewhat rough illustrative tabulation.

Table 2 attempts to show how the person may shift from relative self-reliance to reliance upon others in economic, social, physical, and psychological functioning.

Thus it would appear that with the events called aging—which are losses—there is not so much a rejection and neglect of the older person by the family or the community as there is a greater or lesser capacity of the person to maintain his morale, to want others, to need and seek others, and to be protected from need to call upon others for social, emotional, financial, and physical aid.

This takes us to the last of the three topics: there is little doubt but that many old persons are brought or sent to institutions—they rarely go of their own choice or volition—and that they enter the old-age home, nursing home, or psychiatric hospital with reluctance, bitterness, fear, and anger. They resent the persons who take them there and appear to be sending them away; they fear and resent their potential attendants within the institution, and the institution itself; and they are frightened about, angry at, and ashamed of, themselves for their state of need, their social plight, and their personal helplessness. Is this because they do not understand or appreciate their needs and because our culture, for what were once good reasons that are now outweighed by their bad effects, has impressed upon us an abhorrence for institutions? Or are these persons who are so resentful of the institutional care they appear to need *dependent* persons who are manifesting anger in their search for the relationship they desire, but which they should not?

Have those who are admitted to state hospitals been sent there because they had no place to go in their state of physical, psychological, social, and economic need and inability to care for themselves? In one

Table 2 *From self-reliance to overt dependency with the losses of aging**

Factor	Self-reliance	→				Overt dependency →
Economic	Wages Pension OASI	Dividends Interest Savings	Insurance	Contribution from children	Help from extended family or friends	MAA-OAA
Social	Friends and spouse	Family	Neighbors and community	Special clubs	Day centers	Institutions
Physical and/or	Self	Spouse	Children	Old-age home	Nursing home	State hospital
Psychological	Discriminatory capacity	Well-established mechanisms of psychological adaptation	Well-established mechanisms of social and of emotional adaptation	Family —————→		
				Friends —————→		
				Companions or attendants ————→		
				Nurses and physicians ————→		

* With aging, protective factors may be lost. Table 2 shows how a loss of one or more protective factors can be compensated for by the existence of the others. It must be noted that there are degrees of loss; it is not necessarily all or none. For example, psychological loss may entail, among others, loss of capacity for socialization on the basis of decreased perceptiveness, flexibility, or choice of responses available, and decreased specificity or efficiency of responses. Such loss may not seriously disturb the social functioning of the older person if there are well-established mechanisms of psychological and social adjustment upon which he can rely, good habits of thought, automated and social patterns—courtesy, manners, social grace. Great reliance upon these well-automated functions constitutes a rigid and vulnerable state.

When automated psychological functions dictating good social behavior will not suffice, or are lost, the next compensatory devices are the internal resource we can term automated patterns of emotional adjustment—the automated winning manipulative or controlling modes of social interaction contingent upon the internalized methods of dealing with fear, anger, guilt, and drive for self-assertion. When those in turn fail, the individual is left at the mercy of the communication value of his signs of loss, distress, and need. His needs must then both be recognized and be met by others.

This is crudely demonstrable by the tabulation which, followed from left to right, gives some indication of the shifting of self-reliance—with flexibility and maximal capacity for mastering problems unaided—to increasing rigidity and a need for the assistance of others in few major areas in which loss occurs with aging.

sense this is true: a great many of the aged who reach state hospitals are the socially deprived, the kinwrecked, the poor, who have no family member to turn to in time of need because there are none, or who have only relatives who are so distant geographically or in relationship that it would be illogical under any circumstances to expect intimacy and assistance from them.

What of those who go to nursing homes and old-age homes? Again, there is some truth in the statement that the old persons who go to them do so because of a lack of a properly supportive home and an intimate and concerned family.

However, there is much evidence that families have a highly protective attitude toward the aged in our society. While it may be too early to reach definite conclusions about the meaning of some of the information we have gathered, it appears likely that certain inferences will be supported.

Taking all factors into account, our data suggest that—as measured by institutionalization for brain syndrome, by physical status, and by death rates—the family (husbands, wives, and children) exerts a protective, caretaking influence over aged persons. Families appear to forestall or prevent *long-term* institutionalization of older persons who have disorders most threatening to life by providing care at home or in local general hospitals. Persons who are admitted to institutions when relatively sound, physically or mentally, have been admitted to institutions which promise to be congenial and preservative to social functioning, the old-age homes. Families in our society, contrary to considerable popular opinion and mythology, do appear to nurse the sick and to try to find asylum, comfort, or external aids for parents who are losing resources and need more assistance than they can give.

Our society may be aligning itself on the side of a myth. The myth is that if families were more reverential of the aged, less neglecting, more energetic in their care, then loneliness and boredom would be averted and the deterioration of aging would be slowed or prevented. There is some truth here which must not be lost or forgotten. However, in our society, aged persons do not enter institutions so much because of neglect or rejection as because they are so impaired physically and mentally that they cannot be maintained in the private home. It is true that society has not yet fully recognized or reorganized itself to meet the growing individual and family needs for good institutional care. Consequently there are regrets and self-recriminations in families when it becomes necessary to call upon inadequately staffed and organized institutions. The individual has needs, the family—if there is any—responds as best it can, and the community appears to respond reluctantly, half-heartedly, or with inadequate resources because of inadequate social organization and what this entails—shortages of money, of personnel, of facilities, and of information.

In summary: I have tried to indicate that the subjective factors, loneliness and boredom, are more usually symptoms of personal distress than of a family's neglect; that such symptoms in old age may stem from remote causes—socialization in the early life of the person—and from a lack of personal resources for self-determination and mastery; that families do not seem to be rejecting of their aged; and that our nursing and psychiatric institutions do not appear to be overused or misused. We can do more to reestablish healthy family intimacies and individual independence by expanding and strengthening our agencies and institutions directly or indirectly than by insisting through invoking guilt, shame, or fear that already overburdened family members take on additional tasks. This is a line taken by misguided persons which tends to obstruct what aging and aged persons need more than anything else —that is, the institutionalization of social organizations which are truly preservative and therapeutic and not depreciatory of human morale and dignity. This means that persons should be helped away from guilty, dutiful, binding, unconstructive dependent relationships toward dignified, self-reliant self-sufficiency; that society should support their self-sufficiency by recognition of the right of all persons, including the aged, to the availability of sustaining services and facilities; and that we recognize the need for social attitudes and organization which encourage and enable those who need special services to make use of them in a self-respecting and mutually cooperative fashion.

If the family is to survive as a voluntary organization—to use Dr. Parson's phrase—then, among other things, our society must contribute to family cohesion by helping in the humane treatment of the weak, sick, and aged family members. Otherwise their frightening or burdensome presence and the time, energy, money, and personal interest they require will prevent the adequate socialization of children. More socialization will be toward precocious independence, and pseudo-independent dependency relationships will be the result. By occupying the middle generation the first generation can force the environment to be harsh and depriving for the third generation, who, inadequately socialized, will in turn become highly demanding, dependent persons whose search for parental surrogates from youth to old age will contribute to family—and to social—disruption. We will be continuously occupied with repair, and not with growth.

Reference

1. Obviously, not all the elderly are in good health. Indeed it would be surprising if, by some process of elimination, they were. It is possible that emotional stability may contribute to longevity, but it is also possible that certain types of mental disorder may contribute to long life. It is certain that some persons fail to reach what would otherwise be their maximum potential age because they have directly or very deviously contrived suicide. Nevertheless, within the ranks of elderly persons we find all the behavior disorders of maturity—character disorders, neurotic traits, psychoneuroses, and psychoses. In addition, the many years of life may have bared special personality problems which have injured the integrity, and the capacities for functioning, of the person. Because the aged have lived longer, there has been more time for mistaken self-arrangements to yield their unpleasant ends, for the growth of family strife and friction, for the acquisition of illnesses and for their effects to show. Moreover, there has been time for disease and for aging processes to decrease the efficiency of sensory, motor, cortical, integrative, and homeostatic functions. There has also been time for the loss of family, friends, and, all too often, material resources. These many changes and losses add real limitation to what may be an already considerably crippled functional capacity, and as causes of apprehension and anxiety they cause further limitation by the inhibiting and disorganizing effects of fear. With respect to these losses, we may contrast the well to the ill and indicate that as in so many things in this world: those who have good health seem to hold it and improve it; those in poor health fail all the more.

GENTLE PERSUASION: THE FAMILY
OF THE FUTURE

Moderator: J. Ralph Audy

Dr. Audy brings to this symposium the view of the ecologist, the concept of the "niche" within the environment in which the individual finds himself. His interests in tropical medicine and human ecology have led him to research on typhus and malaria; he has also published studies of groups such as the Kikuyu tribe in Kenya.

Panel Members: Karl H. Pribram, Alvin I. Goldfarb, Judson T. Landis

Dr. Audy Since we are the last panel of the symposium we have the special responsibility of crystallizing the ideas presented. We have three areas of discussion. Firstly, what are the main paths which families are likely to take in the future? Secondly, are any good, bad, or even fatal elements for our society in the different paths? Thirdly, can we or should we do something ourselves either to move away from the bad elements or direct our development toward the things which seem to be good?

I will start with a story which is perfectly relevant and absolutely true; I thought of it when Dr. Landis was talking about the shortcomings in the family.

A number of years ago I visited England and stayed at a guest-house out in the country. It was a lovely house with big gardens, run by a very energetic lady, aged seventy-two. She answered the doorbell one morning, and there at the doorstep was a tiny girl who was the daughter of a neighbor and often played in the garden. The child was holding hands with an even tinier boy at her side. When Mrs. Thomas came to the door, the little girl said in an affected, sophisticated voice, "Oh, good morning, Mrs. Thomas, we have come to tea." So Mrs. Thomas went off to get some cookies and fruit juice, but when she came back there was nobody there. She stepped out and looked along the drive and saw the tiny girl holding the hand of this microscopic boy and running up the drive. She called out, "Come back again: you have not had your tea." The little girl answered, "Oh thank you, Mrs. Thomas, I would simply love to for myself; but I am afraid my husband has wet himself." When I learned of this I couldn't help asking myself, "What is going to happen when that girl grows up, she is married, and her husband disgraces himself, perhaps after a few martinis?" My thought is that she is going to behave in a much less gracious manner.

Now a good deal of this symposium is really concerned with what happens to what we can see in the kind of relationship of these children at play, and what happens in later life in the development of families. When these sweet, lovable youngsters become locked in holy matrimony how are they going to develop in their later life, and what is more, what kind of children are they going to bring up in developing the world?

Behind this symposium was a genuine concern, felt by a very large number of people, that there were plenty of appearances and signs that we should be worried and alarmed at the way in which our family was either breaking up or falling to bits, or at the very least developing along lines which produce many of the problems which have been described during the symposium. We accept the fact we are in a time of transition, and everybody knows that during any time of rapid social change and transition other changes must occur. The pupa of a butterfly looks like a nice, quiet, sleeping pupa, but inside it is simply turmoil with a caterpillar changing into a butterfly. During this particular time of turmoil one wonders what is going to emerge from our social pupa— a butterfly or some horrible little social deformity? A good deal of the future of our society literally depends on this.

There has been a tendency among many of the participants in the symposium to suggest that things really are all right, that we don't really have to worry very much, and that the family is more interesting than it is alarming. But perhaps we are tending to bathe ourselves in security instead of emerging into the hard world of reality with which we have to deal.

Dr. Goldfarb has shown that although economics and, to a lesser extent, social pressures have a very powerful influence on the troubles that beset older people, these troubles nevertheless have their origin primarily in the family failure that develops the individual and relatives socially. One needs to be trained for a happy old age. The querulous and demanding get the negative response which may be expected, and the rejection makes them deteriorate even further. Therefore we can bring the problems of the aged right back to the early family, and I hope Dr. Goldfarb will elaborate further on the child as father of the grandfather. Dr. Smelser presented us with a relative paradox. Because there is less participation by the extended family and by neighbors, the parental responsibility has increased for the early formative years of the child. Yet it is the prevalent complaint that there has been a lessening of moral authority of parents and their ability to mold the basic personality of the child so that he will respect authority.

Dr. Landis viewed this from a different angle. I privately wonder if an element in this paradox is that the young so often are much better informed than their parents, which must lower their respect. Also, the young have become blasé because there are so many advances every year, such as flying to the moon.

However, I should like to start by asking Dr. Landis what he considers some of the essential danger signals in courtship.

Dr. Landis   I think that the way love is pictured to our young people today causes them to conclude that it is a quarreling relationship and that the course of true love never runs smooth, which is simply not true. Actual quarreling in a relationship during dating engagement is indicative of unhappiness and divorce for the young people. If the girl or her family has reservations, they are much more important than how the boy feels about it, and this is definitely a danger signal. The times they have broken up the affair or she has given back the ring all constitute serious danger signals. Then you take a mixture of religion as a danger signal because some young people simply cannot bridge such differences as those between the Catholic and Protestant faiths. These are all illustrations of potential difficulties for the young couple.

Dr. Audy Dr. Pribram, in your description of the multiple-focus family where the focus is shifting from time to time, you mention there is also the possibility of the fall guy, the person who at any given time is going to be chosen in that family without their realizing it for the maximum amount of stress and therefore very often the next person who is going to be admitted to the hospital.

Dr. Pribram That is pretty far from the topic "Commitment to Dreams," but this kind of a shifting-focus notion certainly predisposes to this happening, as it does in any other small group where certain roles are played by particular individuals. This then becomes a role that is the fall guy; the one who is the most pathologically disturbed person plays that role to the hilt. Everyone helps him with it, he takes it, and finally he goes in for treatment. I don't think there is more to be said about that.

Dr. Goldfarb I would like to comment on what you asked Dr. Landis.

I think that there are some danger signals that we all see in impending marriages, which we are often inclined to regard as virtuous and to look upon in an encouraging way. I believe that people who get married to each other should be in love in the best sense, but I am very wary of romantic love. I think that this is a glamorization and idealization of an individual with an expectancy that can never be realized. It actually is a search for a parental figure and these marriages are parentifications. They have their roots early in childhood, and thinking of Dr. Audy's story, I myself would like to see kids not so precociously mature that they tend to marry; what they really want are parents before they get out of their diapers. Such marriages are doomed to end as failures and to make for a sequential polygamy, as one sees among persons where there is unlimited mobility and funds. As one husband decreases in stature and another likely individual is selected, his star rises as the first one falls. There is an exchange, disappointment, another selection, disappointment, another selection; this can go on as long as the selectee will permit himself to be taken in by marriage. Either partner may be involved in this phenomenon.

Dr. Audy Dr. Landis, would you care to discuss the point made before, that one aspect that has been lacking so far in this symposium is the broad aspects of ideology, religion, and morals by which the decisions for the future should be guided.

Dr. Landis I have completed a study of 3,000 families focused upon the religiousness of the family and success in family living as measured by divorce, happiness of marriage, and the conception that children have of themselves—whether they see themselves favorably or unfavorably in many different ways. That research was analyzed by a Catholic, a Protestant, and a Jew, as well as by people of no faith. It showed that the families rated high on religiousness were also the ones with the lowest divorce rate, the highest happiness rate, and where the children viewed themselves most favorably and had to live up to moral standards such as refraining from premarital sex relations more than those where the atmosphere was one of indifference or antagonism to religion. It showed that the families in which there was no religion at all were the ones with the highest divorce rate, most frequent premarital sex relations, the highest unhappiness rate, etc.

This conference has not discussed religion in the family, but I think these facts should be brought out.

Dr. Audy Dr. Krech said earlier that in one study 50 per cent of married females don't read books and also that 13 per cent did not seek intelligence in their husbands. Of course, if they did seek intelligence in their husbands, they probably wouldn't get so many so readily. But it showed by this that there are two areas of confusion. One is that intelligence may be confused with education and book learning and calculated by grade points and semester units in the past. What worries me a little about this is that we are getting clear evidence of some sexual selection. Birds show very obvious sexual selection, picking the best males, and their social machinery is built to this end. It does not seem to apply in the human example, and that is a serious matter because with social changes we are emphatically also getting genetic changes.

The other point is confusing cleverness with wisdom. There are plenty of extremely wise and intelligent people who have hardly read a single book, and it is their kind of wisdom that is needed rather than our present worship of numbers of units we may gain in our so-called education. This is very much tied in with the moral education of youngsters.

From the Floor Are we committed necessarily to a mechanistic model of the family group as a single biological entity or a social unit such as the family? In any event, isn't the structural model, to whatever degree it may be correct, the lesser in importance in assaying the human condition, particularly for the future?

Dr. Pribram The answer is multiple. Firstly, what most scientists mean by a model is just that: something to work with, which can give some kind of understanding and therefore control over what it is that we are modeling. It is a replica but never the identity; however, this is a useful word and concept. The first part of the question sounds as though the commitment is to say, "We are no more than a mechanism or something of that kind," which is really a meaningless kind of statement. A model is mechanistic if it is a computer model, for instance. I am not dealing with two or three hundred computers, but with people. Nonetheless I can learn a great deal about how they solve problems, do mathematical functions, etc., by studying how computers are programmed. The model is a great help.

The rest of the question goes on, "Isn't the structural model to whatever degree it may help"—it says "correct"; whether it matches would be a better way of stating this—"is it of lesser importance in assaying the human condition, particularly for the future?" And here I come to what Dr. Landis said and give you a contrast in our views. I seem surrounded by pessimists, but I am really quite optimistic. I think that if we learn something about the structure of how a family operates, we can ask the right questions, which always comes before solving problems. Dr. Landis made a lovely statement when he said, "The most important product of marriage is children." Maybe it is; maybe it isn't. I would suggest that the most important product of marriage is stability, dreams, and commitment. The children will take care of themselves if these things are properly functioning.

Dr. Landis I think that Dr. Pribram gave the answer to his own question there when he said, "If they are properly functioning." I certainly question, for instance, whether teen-agers can perform these functions adequately. So many of their dreams and commitments are so unrealistic that it is ridiculous to think that they can perform the functions of parents properly.

Dr. Pribram When I think of teen-agers having difficulties, I don't see an easy solution. What has happened is that we have become affluent with respect to our dreams too quickly. Teen-agers have not lived through with us what it takes to produce that dream and lack the whole input before commitment can occur. Perhaps one of the questions that Dr. Landis and Dr. Goldfarb both asked is how can we train our children in dream formation which is appropriate to the kind of world they will be living in when they reach adolescence?

Dr. Goldfarb When I was a student we didn't call it *dream* as such: we used to call it deferring immediate gratification and satisfactions for the sake of later greater pleasure. I still think this is the way to put it. I love to see a nice, dependent, childlike teen-ager who doesn't know how to smoke or drink, and doesn't hang around the house complaining about his studying, but gets on with it instead. I feel less happy about one who has learned to be precociously mature, thinking in terms of marriage because he or she might as well leave this miserable hole of a home and make something better. If you can't do any better and don't have good parents, you should find somebody nice who is going to be good, loving, and kind, and will take care of you and be gratifying as a wife or husband. This is another matter, and I would be in complete agreement with you.

I would also agree with something you said with respect to means and ends which I think is extremely important. Many of these children and adults have taken the means and made an end of them. The ends of marriage will still be the same and will be for a long time; they are still to provide companionship, a readily available sexual partner, to legitimize parentage, make parents responsible for care of children, to guarantee a socializing unit for children, and so forth. The ends of marriage are not particularly to provide a courtship situation in which people are caressing, persuasive, and loving perpetually. This is a means toward seeing that the goals might be achieved, and I personally would like to see teen-agers have a prolonged dependency period so that paradoxically they may become independent, goal-seeking, and able to achieve a goal type of a self-reliant individual.

Dr. Pribram You remember I said that the reversal that takes place at the time of commitment is really a reversal; that is, I view it as a tape which has been going along in the sense of differentiation and now is reversed and played backwards.

Dr. Goldfarb You could demonstrate that in very early socialization in children with respect to the relationship to the mother, in which the mother is mistaken for the food.

Dr. Pribram Exactly. If you have a very short tape before commitment takes place, it is going to run itself off very rapidly, leaving this emptiness you describe, and so the delay.

Dr. Audy To bring these topics on teen-agers into focus, taking a slap at the school, two questions have been directed to Dr. Landis. The first one is, "How influential do you think is Dr. Max Rafferty's critical attitude in preventing family living education from gaining a place in the high school curriculum of the state?"

The second question is, "What practical things can be done to teach school boards of the vital importance of family living classes in high schools?"

Dr. Landis I think that since the launching of the first Sputnik in 1957 there has been a tremendous criticism of our educational system. It hurt our pride to think that the Russians could do something we couldn't. I would say that Dr. Rafferty is simply going along with many others who have been very critical of our educational system. So one may go back to teaching the three R's and some back to teaching of mathematics every year in grade or high school. This suggests in general that those who want to go back to something have been winning out. I have thought this would cease before now, but it is still present. Our job is to educate all youths, not just the few that are going to reach the moon. We shape our curriculum largely for that small group, but most children are not going on to college. I have given the statistics here of what girls do after they graduate from high school. They marry and start having children and that is their life whether we like it or not. The majority of boys are going to marry these girls and are going to be the fathers. We must keep this in mind when we consider the purposes in education. Of course, I agree that we should put more emphasis on the teaching of foreign languages; it embarrasses me to go abroad and find I can't speak two or three languages like so many Europeans can. Still I would say that Dr. Rafferty is simply swept up with many other well-intended people who really do not understand what should be provided for all children.

Now the other question: what can we do as parents, what can be done with the different school boards, and so on? I think that all the studies we have done actually show that parents want the schools to give family life education: there is no argument there. We do find in these studies that administrators are a little hesitant, and you can understand that possibly because it is true for some family courses which include sex education. The administrator is often hesitant to do anything that might cause some maladjusted individual in the community to start a ruckus over the word "sex," and some administrators tend to drag their feet. So I think the answer to the question is the need for enlightenment, for Dr. Rafferty and school boards, and I really don't think Dr. Rafferty would disagree with me at all if he understood. The parent-teacher association and other groups of parents should organize to let the school board know how they feel, and reinforce a timid administrator. This would get action. Actually, until Sputnik, California was doing a great deal in developing good programs of family life education and was one of the leading states.

Dr. Audy   Dr. Goldfarb, does the genetic choice of mate have a feasible future in this country with happiness taken into consideration?

Dr. Goldfarb   That reminds me of what George Bernard Shaw said about the barmaid who would make a much better mother for his children than anyone he could think of, but he was quite convinced she wouldn't make him a good wife.

Genetically speaking, Shaw's barmaid might have produced good, healthy offspring, but she probably would not have had the background and the caliber of mind with which he could have been contented. So there is a little more than simple genetic mixing, unless we get to know so much about DNA and chromosomes that we can predict through a knowledge of the genetic structure exactly which two people would fit. This would be the best kind of matching of computer tapes conceivable.

Dr. Pribram   I would suggest a little delay here in order to get the right matching. Again, if we look at the structures involved and match those as Shaw suggested, rather than looking at the product in the sense of what kind of child is produced, the whole thing would go off much more smoothly. I think that is what normal people tend to do and that it is not quite so bad as all that.

Dr. Goldfarb   I think we tend to forget that about 95 per cent of individual functioning is a product of socialization. We are all pretty much alike. Even variations in intelligence are not so great that they can't be tremendously influenced by cultural forces, and it is this which makes the matching.

Now if somebody will come up with a really good agency that can figure out some of the characteristics you have mentioned, and then give an individual something of a choice out of a selected number, I think it would work. That is what we try to do in our society, seen, for example, when persons of the same religion want to marry each other. We try to help limit the choices of mates on similar backgrounds and training, and then within that group one picks the person one likes, for better or worse, because there are many accidents that can occur after marriage.

From the Floor   Is there not a conflict and inconsistency between the Hippocratic oath and the permissive approach to sexual behavior which was described earlier today, and which by inference is acceptable as being normal?

Dr. Goldfarb   I will answer that first by saying the Hippocratic oath, as I understand it, protects the patient from being taken advantage of by the doctor. I think that a doctor who wouldn't instruct a patient verbally about the proper sexual practices in a proper, tactful, and suitable way at the right time would be taking advantage of the patient. I think that his patients are entitled to sexual information, but it has taken me as much as two or three years of once or twice a week with some people visiting and talking to get to the point where I could begin to tell them some of the facts of life so that they could hear them. They were so frightened and terrified by sex and sexuality that all of the instruction, no matter how clearly, explicitly, calmly, and sensibly put, could not get through, and this is my concern about teaching it in the schools.

I think by the time you try to teach children, the social structure is terrorizing them for a good reason, that they don't get into things too soon they should not be handling. But this is also a culture one is attempting to socialize properly.

Dr. Audy   I can't help but think of the man who went to the psychiatrist to be relieved of his inferiority complex, and after about ten minutes of talk the psychiatrist thought for a moment and said, "I can't do very much for you, I'm afraid: the trouble with you is that you really are inferior." The sexual point is that by the time we get up to high school, or even before then, many people are already so molded or have had so many doors closed in their minds that it is no use saying, "This is the way to do it." The only way to do it is to go further back still so we have the right sort of soil: it is no use to put the seed in the wrong type of soil.

Dr. Pribram   I would like to call attention to the fact that instruction at the verbal level is somewhat different from education. For instance, chimpanzees have to be taught in sexual matters and they don't speak at all. One of the things we primates have to live with is that although the "lower forms" and other forms of life know how to reproduce themselves, primates are not so gifted. They have to be educated, and, of course, a sophisticated member of the other sex is perhaps the best introduction. It is with chimpanzees, but I don't know about humans. So we have a real problem as to whether one talks verbally about these things which can help some, or whether one lets things happen as they will in a society which is geared to a less strict and rigid way of bringing children up.

Dr. Landis   All the research we have done shows that people who do not have premarital sex relations have an advantage in that they get along better in marriage. There is not necessarily a cause-and-effect relationship there because further analysis of those who had premarital sex relations shows they are more apt to be nonreligious and to come from unhappy families or divorced families. So the research is not only on premarital sex but the whole series of other strikes against these people. Whether or not they have had premarital sex they would not have done so well in marriage, and our research is not very satisfactory if you approach it from that point of view.

Dr. Kirkendall's solution for what it does do to a relationship if we do or we don't is a very unrealistic approach. Most men can remember their youth, but would they ask "What is this going to do to our relationship?" in deciding whether they should or should not? I find that women tend to agree with that philosophy, but I have not found very many men who find this a good new standard for what we do and don't do.

In my personal view I don't think there is any doubt but that it is better to wait for marriage. Yet if you look at the statistics, you will find quite a large percentage of engaged couples. At the University of California, where I did my last study, you would find it to be true especially during the latter part of the engagement that they do have premarital sex relations and some quite often. In discussing premarital sex I think you have to classify the different types of premarital experiences. A girl is raped; that is premarital sex, as is incest. Steady-dating affairs that break up are also premarital sex. There is no doubt that the woman is promiscuous in her sexual behavior before marriage. As Dr. Kinsey indicated, women are much more likely to be promiscuous in their extramarital sex behavior.

Dr. Goldfarb To me this is really interesting and points up the difficulties that we have all experienced in bringing the information of two disciplines together. As I hear you talk about sociologic data, they become to me clusters that would probably be associated with what I call certain intrapsychic experiences or psychodynamics. I wonder whether agreement of these things that you have described from the sociological point of view might not be found to almost exactly parallel what I was talking about as a socialization-type school: the person who is socialized very adequately for a certain kind of society in which one would find all of these things that you mentioned in homeostatic mechanisms, occasional rapes, occasional incests, and certain kinds of needs for external rather than internal policing forces in terms of particular types of conscience structures. Have you been able to make such parallels between people and their search for parent substitutes and people to live with, and so on?

Dr. Landis I don't know that I have specifically worked on that, but the more research I do, the nearer we move in that direction. Going back to premarital sex in our studies, we used to take such facts as were they virgins or weren't they? And that was the research. Now as we analyze the data more and more and get the background factors, we find that there are a whole constellation which tie together and determine whether the person makes a success of marriage or not, and you can't isolate one of these factors.

Here is another type of research we used to refer to, going back to religion. People who get married in a church service are much more apt to stay out of the divorce court and have a happier marriage; therefore get married in a church. It might be determined that way, and yet what we know as we analyze the data now is that the people who have a church wedding are more apt to have come from a happy family, not a divorced family. These young people are more apt to have met in church rather than a saloon or some place like that; they had a long engagement, which our research shows is predictive of a happy marriage; and the parents approved of the marriage—there is a whole constellation of factors that go together.

Dr. Goldfarb They are people who have been encouraged in their development to form a kind of inner constellation so that they really want to do and enjoy doing what they have to do.

Dr. Landis That is right.

Dr. Pribram They have become habituated.

Dr. Audy Premarital sex has always existed, but it seems to be increasing greatly. Elsewhere in this symposium it has been brought out that it is only one symptom of a general problem expressing itself in many different ways, of which increasing premarital relationships and a lowering of what we commonly regard as moral standards is becoming more and more prevalent. On the whole the basis for behavior that we regarded as commendable in the past is—now and in the future—that more people should have more self-respect, more respect for others, and also a little more self-discipline. Perhaps one of the problems we have to deal with is how to get more of this into younger people before they get channelized in other directions.

Dr. Landis I can get very discouraged and pessimistic about the future of the family when I look at the number of disturbed families and children in society.

I get encouraged, though, with conferences of this type. I think that the truth will make us free. I think that we do not know the truth about marriage and parenthood, and most people don't. In mentioning that statistic that half as many divorces take place in California each year as marriages, I shock many people. It is published in the papers every once in a while and it should be shocking. The illegitimacy rate shocks people and yet that again has received great publicity. But I think if we have more conferences of this type, put them on the air and on television so people can know what the score is, and sell the books that will come out of these conferences, it will help.

I think if we can just put a fraction of the effort and money into helping the family do better that we're putting into going to the moon, then I would become an optimist, I think.

Dr. Pribram I will second that. The very fact that we are alarmed is perhaps the most optimistic note that we can sound because with understanding will come change and commitment.

Dr. Goldfarb I was not joking when I said in my talk that I am not particularly optimistic about the chance that the family will survive in a form that we would like to see.

When I first went into practice and saw people, I said, "Well, the public is at least twenty-five years behind the times and new ideas have not yet reached them. When these young people that I am now seeing as my patients have had their children they will be different." I am now seeing their children: they are just as terrorized with ideas that sex is dirty and violent and sinful, just as uninformed, just as unable to gain pleasure independently in ways that we have incompletely described. This disappoints me. It is the disillusionment of middle age, I suppose, and this is my problem to work out; but it is not one that makes for optimism.

Further, with the population explosion, we're not becoming just short of food; we're getting shorter and shorter of schools, teachers, and of socializing influences that we depended upon in the past. Parents are not socializing influences, as we point out. Ministers, the police, nurses, doctors, and peer groups are those who have great socializing influences. So I expect that there will be a lot more illegitimate pregnancies, more so-called juvenile delinquency; that the suicide rate will continue to remain high or will go up; that the United States may slip with respect to infant mortality even more than it has; that our death rates will not be as good as they were in the past; and that our longevity will come down. Unless we do something along the lines of social organizations toward correcting the kind of socializations taking place, the family will be different and the world in which we live will not be as nice a place as it could be.

Dr. Audy We have agreed generally, I think, that the family is going to survive because there are some definite reasons for its permanent perpetuation at least in some elements of it. But we are alarmed very much about what this family is going to develop into in the future, and the way and the kind of society this is going to produce.

On the good side we are certainly considerably informed, which we were not before; what is better, we are rapidly learning more.

Secondly, we do recognize that we must go back to earlier stages of individual life all the time in order to give the sort of education and moral direction that we would like to. But we can't do it with the wrong sort of material and we can't put the seed in the wrong sort of soil.

Also, we are greatly improving communication; I think this is another very good point for the future and I hope that these good points will gradually help to balance this alarm which we most certainly do feel.